TRIUMPH

THE JOURNEY TO UNDERSTANDING THE SELF

By

Dwayne Gavin

Powerful lessons filled with personal insight and skills to develop one's awareness of clarity about the inner self and beyond.

© Copyright, 2012

By

Dwayne Gavin

ISBN-978-0-9852206-1-7

Library of Congress Number: 2012912312

All rights reserved. No part of this publication may be reproduced, stored in a retrieval system, or transmitted in any form or by any means—electronic, mechanical, photocopying, recording, or otherwise—without the prior written permission of the copyright owner and publisher.

Cover design by Dominion Multi-Media, Tallahassee, Florida

Photography by Phillip Williams

Editors:

Jacqueline Harper
Brenda Smith, Ph.D.

DG PUBLISHING HOUSE, INC.
5322 Mimosa Circle
Lake Park, GA 31636
www.dgpublishinghouse.com
850-566-8169

Preface

Knowing how to observe motions within the inner self and having a readiness to believe that only ignorance about understanding inner impulses are the causes which prevent you from moving on beyond your past to reach new awareness. You can become your own next master – TRIUMPH!

Triumph is unfolding clarity that invites you to examine the truth about your inner self; the motions of your life are what you may find in it. Over time, there are so many pieces of motions inhabiting your inner self and to my discovery such motions are the real driving forces behind your joy, pain, feelings, and thoughts.

The Triumph

I welcome you to discover many of the motions within and, to some degree, pull the cover off of those motions so that there is clarity about the various disguises that once kept you blind to the real source of growth, enlightenment and change. I address what I term to be the "inner self," the one to face should there be an elimination of ignorance about why thoughts, feelings and emotions are most important to observe and how you can take control over inner motions to bring about the changes that you need for any real triumph in your life. I invite you to see yourself for what you have become and/or what you can become as you become insightful of your inner self.

What is most rewarding is feared the most, in terms of taking control of oneself in a germane way. This book encourages you to choose a readiness to rearrange yourself internally to become driven with a new clarity with which to transform yourself with a brand new

The Triumph

understanding which will empower you to become happy in every aspect of your life. Moreover, the triumph emphasized in this book is a type of awareness that enables you to see any distraction of real motions within. Thus, you will find in this book an understanding of a human being's inner vibrations and skills with which to enhance you to live in a state of happiness and contentment. All in all, reading this book will teach you how to prioritize your thoughts, feelings, and emotions.

Identification of emotional awareness and the experience of power over your emotions are in some way the triumph that is explored in this book. Lastly, many of the personal experiences that have been shared in this book are somewhat spiritual, even the beginning of what I term to be the turning point toward triumph.

Acknowledgment

I wish to acknowledge Global Christian Church, Willyoung Alexander, Janis Gavin Terry, Roland Terry, Christine White, Michael Powell, Walter White, Derrick Crawford, Dorothy Barnes, and my entire family. I especially wish to acknowledge my editors: Ms. Jacqueline Harper and Brenda Smith for all the time invested into this book to make it available to you.

Introduction

There are important factors which embrace triumph. Many of them are characterized by high spiritual, moral, or intellectual worth. In the natural process relative to self awakenings, most people, if not the vast majority of persons, are not able to attain majestic and/or character of nobility. Without having triumphed at some point in their lives, it would be unlikely for them to rebound once wounded emotions from below the threshold of conscious perception until transformation. Adequate factors having enabled them to produce states of awe and awareness within the self lead them to be triumphant. What is important, you must reach a state of awareness to always recover from emotional deficiency. There is only one underlined enemy to triumph. In many cases if not every case, that enemy is very

The Triumph

hard to recognize. It is subtle. It is called ignorance. Ignorance in any area of your intellect often poses itself as a type of disguise, even subliminal when adequate awareness is needed to prevent you from experiencing emotional debilitation and/or immobilization.

The surest way to victory is to become insightful of what you have allowed emotionally to wrap around your inner self. It is wise to be able to identify your inner motions. Maybe, for some people prayer and for others meditation seems to be a resource to reveal all of their inner motions. Arguably, both are resources. On the one hand, I have found it to be previous experiences from the past. On the other hand, knowledge is an excellent resource with which to obtain victory.

Knowledge from textbooks seems to be most common among intellectuals, not to mention the lasting biblical quotation, "My people perish because of the lack of knowledge."

The fact is that not all persons are alike intellectually;

The Triumph

therefore, buying any number of textbooks to read isn't for all, so this means that studying oneself is the best possible way to triumph. There are countless ways, for sure, to triumph but none faster than observing your inner self relative to how you interact with every motion in your life, including people, places and things.

For example, the emotions of relationships, desirable cravings, and addictions are motions. Motions are only movements occurring within the self prompting you to give feeling, so that you describe what priority they have in your life. All motions when described and given positions of priority among other motions that you carry become emotions to deal with eventually. It is my personal experience that emotions naturally compete for first place in your life. They must be handled and daily monitored with keen awareness.

Some can be tamed; others must be cut out all together before the triumph. The reason that motions are subliminal is because of their

The Triumph

disguised and covered up descriptions and the self worth that you give them. The real reality of triumph is that you cannot deal with your weakness until you are ready to see your inner self for what you have over the period of your life arranged it to be.

No battle with your demons, no contest with another, none of your struggles with others can be defeated by physical means. Instead, triumph comes only when you reorganize, reprioritize, realign, and reprogram your inner self because your inner self resides in a physical body. From birth, it is often given many instructions, such a broad curriculum and many lessons, until it becomes so vast that if not observed, it functions as energy and/or a fire out of control, if uncontrolled. The triumph is the self having reached awareness to control every living motion that makes up the inner self; thus, your life is redirected from acting out in ignorance. It is as if you have been given a new life. Old things are long gone to return no more. The only new phenomenon left is triumph.

This book is dedicated to the Rev. Dr. Landon Alexander who has been a voice of higher consciousness for me on my path to triumph! Special thanks given to Addie Smith, my late great grandmother, for my spiritual background. I also appreciate my parents and each of my readers. My hope is that this book leads you to your personal triumph.

Contents

1. Discovering the True Enemy
2. The Awakening
3. Your Brilliance
4. Ask, Seek, and Knock
5. Defeating Your Demons
6. The Worst Evil
7. You Don't Have to Fear Evil
8. What Plays to My Heart's Breaking
9. Emotions: The Big Conflict
10. Subliminal Seduction
11. The Instructor Who Never Leaves You
12. The Reason for the Journey

13. There Are Seasons in Your Life

14. Discipline

15. Handing Over the Kingdom of Heaven

16. Triumphant

1

DISCOVERING THE TRUE ENEMY

If I don't know myself what I am, I am ignorant of myself, what my purpose is, what my direction is; therefore, how can I say what my true enemy is or isn't? For that reason I must know what truly exists within me so that I may know my enemy.

Suppose that you are born and sent on a journey with little or no knowledge about you, what your purpose is, what direction to

Discovering the True Enemy

pursue meaningful knowledge, except of course, the Bible, the Quran, the Tao, the Torah, or some Hindu Mysticism. All of these teachings may be able to draw you closer to knowing certain truths handed down through the years as an account of history about how other people before you became acquainted with finding for themselves a higher meaning and purpose for their lives.

    Without a doubt, there can be many ways to identify yourself with the experiences of others, and there is no certain way for anyone to get understanding for much needed answers about what you are and where you are to go in your life. It is, however, necessary to have the knowledge about what truly exists within your individual conscious, so that you are not ignorant about who you are, what you are to do with your life, and how to recognize your enemy. Your enemy has always been you not knowing when you have need for knowing. Chances are that there is something that every one of us needs to know individually about our unique purpose, and I am

Discovering the True Enemy

here to tell you that it's findable. It is the knowledge of triumph that you are here to find.

So many times you are distracted from the awareness of triumph seemingly at the time that you need it most. I can tell you why: it's the natural nature of human beings to dismiss challenge to higher consciousness, which I believe is the awakening of what you are ignorant and finding out of what you are really made. Your enemy is revealed when you gain consciousness of your inner self. Your eyes, therefore, awaken to what's your triumph but you don't have it all at once. Instead, you have gotten closer to finding out the ignorance that plagued you for a while.

At the beginning of the triumph, still your direction is not clear although you have just learned the most valuable asset to the triumph being higher consciousness. What is certain, higher conscious is like helium in a balloon without any size to it, the more you try to see its size the higher it goes.

At least as for now, you know that there is something about you that can carry you as

Discovering the True Enemy

high as you need to go, but still your direction about what to pursue must become keener. Next to your enemy is its cousin distraction, from knowing your higher consciousness. Of course, all those seemingly sacred religions play a major role in the distraction. I can tell you why. It is because distraction wants to keep you confused about your path in life. Isn't that the truth?

    Just when you become so overwhelmed about the power of higher consciousness, there comes into play all these religions from which to choose. What a mess to sort out rings out loudly in your mind. Wow, the first test for your brand new higher conscious is there to expose that you really have made some steps near, but you have not yet figured it out. It's designed that way to keep you engaged on your journey! There is a particular line of understanding to be gotten from all the religions, even every spiritual teacher, Guru, Saint, god and/or minister. We are now arriving but still quite slowly. The reason making sense of what religion belongs where, in the priority position of your

Discovering the True Enemy

mind is so mind – boggling is because there is some truth in all of them. Your goal must never be to sort the religions out in terms of priority in your mind, instead appreciate the truths found among all of them.

The reality of all religions is that they in some way account for bringing all people to where they are now, relative to knowing the Divine. Your next step then is to now assess the Divine for yourself since what others discovered is not your very own discovery. This is probably a major setback for you because you think it will take a lot of work, and it is not worth your time to deal with it or maybe you ought to leave it to the mystics to handle, so that you go on with your life care free without having to deal with it. Let me tell you, even a fool could not disagree with you, but it's not the way your life is planned.

Your enemy wants you to run away from challenge when it comes to your getting closer to your responsibility to creation. You are placed as a part of a matrix to find out certain things and leave them behind in the grand scheme of the

Discovering the True Enemy

human being so that mankind can find its way back to its Creator. Just as you had nothing to do with showing up here as a person, you had nothing to do with the arrangement of the matrix. God did! I know what you are thinking now. Why does God act that way? I can tell you why. In the Bible, there were questions raised about God's ways, the same as there were questions in all the sacred texts of the world about God's ways.

Well, I am sorry to inform you as Isaiah the prophet discovered when speaking from his higher conscious, with God's permission, I believe these words, "My thoughts are not your thoughts, my ways are not your ways." I can perceive what you may be thinking now. That is not good enough for me. Rightfully so! God knows! God would say to you," I believe, "Didn't I just tell you that you would not agree?" Let me help you. The whole notion about God's allowing you to know in part is so that you will be surprised about certain occurrences which will happen along your destiny.

You may say, "Well, why do I need to be surprised?" I can answer that for you. If there

Discovering the True Enemy

were no new findings in the human being plight, we would opt to be something other than human beings because we are built and driven by curiosity. Your life would be meaningless, and you would rather die than live if you felt trapped in a realm with any intervention.

What you must know about higher consciousness is that it exists within you although it must be awakened by both good and bad things. Likely, because you are a person with dual natures, both good and bad, your erroneous understanding and ignorance about these two natures separate you from the true reality of them, and what you become is single-focused, leaving you with prolonged understanding which often becomes your enemy.

If you cannot find out what restricts you from higher consciousness, it becomes your enemy because you don't know for which you are here, you don't know your responsibility, and ultimately, that defines a lost identity. How many people do you know enjoy being lost? This is not what life is about; rather the journey that leads

Discovering the True Enemy

everyone to understanding that they are not lost is the mission of the church and/or spiritual institutions. Increasingly, the law is creeping back, seemingly to the front stage battling for a place in our minds with an emphasis to be revered, but there can be no real evidence that laws are the answer for higher awareness because every time a new leader emerges in the free world, you can bet that there will be new laws, policies and restrictions along with him. All in all, finding out the truth about you really is the first insight to triumph. What you are not is a self without purpose. You were born to strive with an intention to reach the goal set for you. No one is born without purpose. Your purpose becomes clear to you after you discover your inner self. Try to see it this way; there is something that you feel connected to with a real passion, but always something that you read into, look into or just have heard seems to challenge you to walk away from it. I am here to tell you, do not run away from it. Seek it! There is an insight that it holds just for you. Just remember,

Discovering the True Enemy

Everything that you take into your higher conscious-spirit cannot escape from being revealed to you. Nothing about seeking yourself can harm you; rather it will release insight that you will need for the awareness for triumph to come for you. Learned behavior is likely the cause of your fears about your higher self, rather than to see your inner self as the nature of God but only a little lesser than God entirely.

    Now you have the first understanding about getting closer to knowing yourself. What you are not is nothing, instead, a real person with a role to play out the next dimension in your life and the lives to come. You are no longer ignorant of the first principle of discovering beginner's knowledge. The reality of heightened awareness about your direction is cut out for you. It is part of your destiny to discover yourself first in life. Finding your way to that answer leads you to triumph. If it is one thing that you must know about yourself, it is that you were made just a little lower than an angel. You may be saying", Wow! How so?" I can tell you how it is so. You

Discovering the True Enemy

see, there was a man in search for God's heart many years ago; his name was David. He became king of Israel before Christ came to his people to show them how God felt about them, with what manner of love God reserved for them, and to what distance God was willing to go to reach them, even save them. David asked God a serious question.

I believe that David asked the right question for all of us. God, as I have said, releases insight to one person for all persons present and persons to come. The question that David asked God is, "What is man, that thou are art mindful of him? And the son of man, that thou visits him? Surprisingly, something happened for human beings. Out from nowhere, words filled David's heart from higher conscious. The conscious of God within him released these words, "Man was made a little less than I am, even lower than an angel and crowned with glory and honor." By God's releasing the abundant truth, the entire creation became closer to knowing what God thinks about all people. God had begun to open up to David

Discovering the True Enemy

deep insight for everyone. God knew that it was the right time to release awareness and insight about us. So God continued that dialogue with David's heart saying, "I made you to have dominion over all the works of creation. Every man being the same, except there must be order among you." David had yet more thoughts racing through his mind. He thought, "When I considered thy heavens, the work of thy fingers, the moon and the stars, which thou has ordained, you mean even I am as creative as these." God's answer was, "Yes, and it's the responsibility of man to put all lesser creatures under his rule, for you are equal with me, only not to me."

What an infusion rushed David's heart! He began to sing for himself the song of God, that others may know that God is excellent, and we must realize that we have similar potential. David sang the song, O LORD, how excellent is thy name in all the earth! Who has set thy glory above everything, yet thou out of my mouth, thy has ordained strength". David was simply overjoyed

Discovering the True Enemy

having gotten closer to what we all must find out about ourselves and God.

Having arrived here, following this initial insight leads to the next insight about triumph. Discovering your true enemy is a process, but it doesn't have to be life long, rather it's your readiness and willingness to ask yourself the right questions that expedite awareness of your ignorance which is the enemy. Most of the time, it requires your being honest with yourself to really see what lies beneath your skin. Thus, when you are truthful to yourself, you release your conscious bringing out more truth because you are ready to face it. Until we truly become ready to confront ourselves about all that is in motion within us, triumph awaits.

Once you are sincere with yourself, there exists a quality of integrity that evolves, and it will work for you rather than against you in pursuit of triumph. No one really knows you truly until you are frank with yourself, and being frank with

Discovering the True Enemy

yourself is always part of the process of reaching triumph, but there are yet more findings to attain triumph. Let us see what those other findings are.

Discovering the True Enemy

2

THE AWAKENING

Once I allow my ignorance to be replaced by awareness to equip me, I am recovered with understanding that releases knowledge to empower me.

It is likely that when you were born no one told you that you were destined to perish should you not obtain all there is to know about yourself and later as much as you needed to know about the Creator. The fact is that very few may have been given this challenging task at birth with the exception of certain ones born to teach the world about higher reality and the afterlife. Those

The Awakening

certain ones born and given at birth their destinies were chosen, and everyone else is called at a certain time to deal with what I term to be the big ignorance.

So there is no need for you to feel as if you are any different from just about all the people born on this planet. It is not your fault that no one set out for you a destiny to fulfill. It was probably best that your parents and/or teachers left it for you to find out the meaning of your life. All people are part of a higher consciousness. Your parents were assigned to you instead of your selecting them. To no surprise, all of us were born prey to the big ignorance, and, therefore, we became students of learned patterns of thoughts, feelings, behavior, and perception. All of which are necessary. Those learned patterns, nevertheless, were likely to embrace the socio-political and religious culture to which you were born. The power of your awakening has nothing to do with which culture you embrace. Neither does it have much to do with the family to which you were born. Nor is it about the socio-political climate

Discovering the True Enemy

that you embrace. Instead, awakening is individual heightened consciousness of the ultimate one reality.

Everyone born of man has a responsibility and role to play in order for the one reality to become all of our shared reality. The reality is named triumph. You have a task to perform to bring yourself and everyone else closer to attaining the triumph.

The road leading to the triumph is plagued with ignorance, and you must be the one to turn yourself over to the voice of higher consciousness which comes to release you from the big ignorance. Fear of going beyond what your first instructors taught you reinforces subtle ignorance and prevents you from the individual triumph assigned to your life. The road of the triumph starts with erasing all fears. Going beyond your fears is the beginning of turning over ignorance, and what you will find on the other side of ignorance is enlightenment, thus, the path to triumph. Ignorance once revealed by the voice in front of higher consciousness is dismantled.

Discovering the True Enemy

Its being once your real enemy can no longer plague you with death threats in your thoughts, feelings, perceptions, and emotions of fear. It is said that Abram, a character mentioned in the Bible, was chosen to go beyond his fears of leaving behind his initial birth culture. When Abram thought about it seriously, God spoke to him through the voice of higher consciousness saying, "Fear not, I am thy shield," thus lessening his fears. Likely, to some this would be insane or too much for God to ask any man, but it brought those within creation once again closer to finding out the one reality to be attained by all men because it puts in motion triumph.

God's voice is the voice of higher consciousness and the only form of true inner peace and protection from the big ignorance. After you have turned over your ignorance to a higher voice of your higher consciousness, there come whisks of awareness that hand over higher meaning for your life in every area.

Any resistance to going beyond your fear is a setback towards triumph. All resistance to move

Discovering the True Enemy

past any ignorance is associated with anxiety which has to be eradicated from your memory so that you keep the course of the triumph. I am here to tell you from my experiences of fear that at any time during my life, my setback has always been because of my lack of knowing what I needed to know at such time about how to solve my own anxiety and inner conflict.

You are no different! Wow! Now you have it, another truth that is released for the purpose of understanding the damage that ignorance poses. A year ago, it is reported that God through the voice of higher consciousness brought again the creation closer to the one reality for everyone-triumph, when a man seeking after the knowledge of God's love for human being explained that God would not have us to be ignorant about our morality. I take this to mean that ignorance must be destroyed in the process of triumph. I am that man to whom God spoke. We perish when we lack knowledge!

There are many forms of education. The most important education is a discovery of your inner self or as one man puts it, your inner man. Nothing about seeking to know your inner self is

Discovering the True Enemy

harmful. Instead, it's quite rewarding and beneficial to recovering you from the big ignorance. Thus, in doing so, you will connect with insights about every person, including yourself.

And once again, you will be the one to bring the creation closer to the one reality of triumph which everyone seeks. The higher you aspire to reach new awareness to recover the world from ignorance, the better the world can be. We are all contributors or should be, to the triumph.

Opening yourself up to the awakening is the joy felt as one's awareness carries one past his natural impulses. The more you use your imagination to come up with a perspective to go past established boundaries for you, the more of a forthcoming abundance of new interpretation and new solutions.

This is how the triumph expands in the areas of focus in your life. The awakening does for you something very rewarding, and the single-most important satisfaction it gives is peace. The triumph is discovered in every area of your life that causes you to forego your pride and in most cases your personal ignorance so that you mentally welcome recreation of yourself internally

Discovering the True Enemy

via alterations in your perception. In my life, I have seen the big ignorance destroy many people, even take their lives.

The big ignorance is the reason for so many divorces, church splits, murder, war and rumors of war, and the difference between the haves and have not's in virtually every culture on the planet. I have heard many people say, "What you do not know can't hurt you." I beg to differ. What you do not know will cost you, even your life. Just think about it. Only technological advances are the result of medicine, education and growth. All these advances are designed to bring us to triumph.

More than two thousand years ago, there was reported a man who possessed many dialects, likely an apostle or follower of Jesus Christ, who discovered something very pertinent about the triumph. While most of his spiritual life, he endeavored with so many Godly people that were for sure zealous of God, he reported that their zeal was not according to the knowledge of God-the triumph.

The man would later discover after spending time with them that they had been consumed by the big ignorance. Finally, all he

Discovering the True Enemy

could do for them was to intercede with God's voice in the higher consciousness in prayer so that he could be of more help. This would be for him, the surest assurance towards an awakening he believed. After much spent time speaking and preaching, he did convince a few of a more excellent way of perceiving God. His last words of prayer for those people were, "Brethren, my heart's desire and prayer for Israel is that they might be saved, for they have a zeal of God but not according to knowledge. They being ignorant of God's righteousness have gone about to establish their own righteousness and not submitting unto God." These are the words in the Apostle Paul's prayer unto God for Israel.

    I might add, people wanting to find the triumph must dissolve their ignorance by submitting unto God's voice of higher consciousness, the spirit which releases awareness above their ignorance. Peace is the reward that comes with your awakening from the big conflict of the plague of ignorance. Peace is the most rewarding benefit of the triumph because it comes from God's voice in the higher consciousness.

    Peace is released only when you become

Discovering the True Enemy

awakened once you become straight up with your inner self about truth. It is my experience that when you find the higher consciousness which God gives you, the more you seek it, the higher it takes you in the triumph. The fact is if you do not determine for yourself what restricts you from higher consciousness, you will miss the triumph. The awakening via higher consciousness keeps you from blaming everyone and/or everything other than your real enemy, ignorance. The big ignorance serves as your distraction from the voice of God found in the higher consciousness. Ignorance anywhere is a threat to triumph there also!

As you move on with your life, just remember that you are part of all of us sent here to help bring the whole creation closer to finding the insights of the triumph, which are scattered all over our being to bring us to its one reality. The triumph is different from religion because it cannot divide us; instead, it releases us from religion and brings us to ourselves. The triumph is designed to propel the inner self to its complete height. The triumph is the journey split into three paths: awareness, understanding and knowledge. Then, only then, can we erase the big ignorance.

3

YOUR BRILLIANCE

Considering I find exceptional clarity about myself and agility of intellect and intervention, my triumph awaits me.

Your brilliance makes the difference between succeeding and possibility. Among rewards in life, nothing can take the place of your mind's reaching grander states of clarity; nor can anything compete with the joy that whisks of clarity bring into your mind. In the process of the triumph, you will begin to discover intellectual brilliance.

The more you find exceptional clarity about your life you will start to view clarity as a technique provided by your inner awareness. Whenever you come to cross roads on your

Brilliance

journey of triumph, only germane clarity can rescue you. It is there to reveal your own brilliance. Anytime you are seeking advanced insight into the secret power of the world, you are showing your brilliance.

It is said this year that there is a shift consciousness present in the world. Modern day apostolic preachers and life coaches are prophesying an outpouring of higher power and advanced happenings which will come all over the world supposedly bringing complete clarity to all people about what God is doing right now. By now you may be saying, "If that is true, I will believe it when I see it." The truth is God is not upstairs playing checkers as some suppose Him to be according to our moves in the world.

Surely, the only way to see what is the result of spirit-higher consciousness is to take on its nature! To me, that is the role of your very own brilliance. There are all sorts of predictions about the shift generation. The awareness that the shift generation is supposed to bring is composed of many things. For example, I am told the clarity of the shift culture will bring the creation once again to the one reality-triumph. I am aware of the shift

Brilliance

coming, and you must be, too. In the process of time, it will come. I believe that as each generation becomes wiser, two things happen: first, the creation comes closer to the one reality—triumph; second, every generation has its own assignment that is designed to discover more of the insights into triumph than the previous generation. Simply, this demonstrates the brilliance of God!

One day while visiting my cousin Derrick Crawford in Orlando, Florida, I was privileged to go to a church only to find two guys talking about the shift culture. Those men were quite insightful about the subject matter. I, at the time, was visiting and not expecting anything but worship. What I remember is that one guy said, "The shift in consciousness is the whole matter." I agreed! The other guy interviewing the guy who had just revealed the secret insight was astonished. I then realized that once again another secret of the triumph was released during the two guys' dialogue. They both went on to say that the shift consciousness would be detected between the ages of 19 to 39.

What is more, these persons are supposed to be wrapped with potential, capacities, and

Brilliance

abilities unseen, unheard, unknown, untapped, unrevealed, unborn, and undone. You would have to agree with these guys that if any group of people are inventors of a new way of thinking, it is definitely younger minds. Those guys reminded me of a series of divine scriptures quoted in the Bible that says, "Eye hath not seen, ear hath not heard and neither has it entered into the hearts of men those things which God has prepared for them that love him." And, God shall reveal all these things in the spirit, voice of higher consciousness. At the time of these forthcoming events, I add that God shall inspire, equip, and create new awareness and triumph once again that will bring the entire creation to the reality of the triumph.

During my youth, I was certainly filled with new ideals that I believed to be right although at times my parents thought differently; thus, real brilliance is that which is different. Brilliance is part of engaging change from the old to the new! Let me tell you, I already see the shift culture present through social media. Because of my being part of the new shift in consciousness, I am doing things I have envisioned: writing books.

Today, I now own a publishing company

Brilliance

due to higher consciousness for which I am put here. And, yes, God inspires me to write so that I am playing a role in the shift consciousness to reveal new insights that will bring the creation closer to the one reality-triumph! Your brilliance comes from your inner state's relating to the inherent ability or capacity for growth, development, or realization to enhance or increase a shift in consciousness. Too many times all of us have not used our maximum brilliance. It is within us to reach an innate potential to absorb from the higher consciousness the power to learn how to develop and accomplish the triumph. In the triumph what unfolds is a new way of replacing your old thinking in order that you see yourself getting closer to the God consciousness.

Thus, your brilliance offers brand new skills to reposition your inner self. Equally important, changes occur as thought alteration which comes to empower you with an understanding of how to recreate your perspective about what should and should not happen in your life. I met Landon Alexander approximately three years ago at the General Missionary Baptist Convention of Georgia.

I am on a different assignment presently. Along the way of my triumph, I noticed that Mr.

Brilliance

Landon Alexander was the Reverend Dr. Landon Alexander. I was impressed by what he was doing with his talent above sixty years of age. He had written 13 books, all of which were on his table as beautiful as any books I have seen, and he along with his wife and son were among the best vendors present at the convention. At the time, I was in the process of getting published my first book. I had no clue of the cost for publishing a book other than a price quoted from a publisher.

Being a new author I was excited about seeing my work in print. After sharing my ambition to publish a book with Dr. Landon Alexander, he made himself available to me for directions on publication. The single most important piece of advice he gave was, "Publish your own book, retain all your royalties, and do it cheaper." "What a nightmare! I thought". Quickly, the voice of God through higher consciousness whispered, *"You can do it because I have prepared Alexander's heart to help you."* I did not question that insight. I knew that the Rev. Dr. Landon Alexander was the vehicle chosen to bring me closer to the meaning of my own life as I had assured myself that I am put here on earth to record my insights and place them in books. The

Brilliance

whole point for meeting Dr. Landon Alexander was that I become closer to the one reality—triumph, in that, God wants me to move on to a higher consciousness so that I might through writing bring the whole creation itself closer to the one reality.

The relationship with Alexander and me grew. I was able to build my own Publishing House and publish my books and others. The greatest thing that he could ever have done for me happened in a single moment through a whisk of awareness. It came as a shift in consciousness and from that moment on, I was off to the races writing and publishing books. Because Dr. Alexander had something to do with my reaching a higher awareness greater than my own, I am doing great things for the whole creation. Today, I call the Rev. Dr. Landon Alexander "Alexander, The Great" because he helped me to do something great. I believe that all of us are responsible for each other in some global way to bring ourselves together as one family with one motivation which is the triumph. One day while talking on the phone with Alexander, I was able to detect a shift in his consciousness as he was giving me advice about life. I said to him, "Sir, you have

Brilliance

dual natures." "He said to me, "What do you mean?" I said, "I can tell when Rev. Dr. Landon Alexander is speaking and when Alexander, The Great as I called it is speaking." He became silent. He, at that time recognized, too, that he had a shift in consciousness when he talked with me in contrast with talking to someone else in general.

I believe from my experiencing heightened consciousness that when someone is to be recovered with understanding, empowered with awareness, and equipped with the knowledge that you have to offer them, you too, are very aware of your very own shift in consciousness as you begin to share it with your devotees. All of us are capable of brilliance. I believe the reason is because man was made in the image of God, after God's likeness and brilliance. Have you ever paid any attention to the way your being functions? If not, you should. It has a perfectly brilliant way about itself. Your brain is hard wired with energy that is electric. It sparks your thoughts. It is your very own command and control center. In fact, it is your commander. Your body is a little universe that responds to the brain being its commander. Each time your brain recognizes a cut on your body, it commands your white blood cells to go

Brilliance

and fix the problem.

Your white blood cells are guards that fight to death to rid your body of infection, to close your wounds and protect your immune center. Your body is always fighting for you even when you don't know or see it. Germs are your adversaries. The same way that your being is functioning in a brilliant manner, so does a shift in consciousness bring about brilliant sparks of awareness to protect your being from mental germs in order to keep you alive for the triumph. Your brilliance is attached to a shift in consciousness, and, therefore, you become closer than you have ever been to the one reality— triumph!

4

Ask, Seek, and Knock

If I question my purpose in life, I can disassemble into parts my ignorance and discover what I am to be.

There are many discoveries unborn, and therefore, countless pages unturned toward the triumph. Because we are all presently on the journey to triumph, we are fulfilling each other's journey. People all around the world need each other in a divine way. Even from childhood, everything that I was taught was the result of someone else's experience and/or learned behavior. Thus, over the period of years, I have become nothing but everyone else's memory of their experiences.

As children growing and progressing toward

Ask, Seek, and Knock

adulthood, the instructions of adults were not questioned. Then all at once, all of us about the age of eighteen discovered that we had a choice in terms of what we could do with our individual minds. You know what happened then I suppose—drama! Next, you seemed to think that you knew more than your parents and teachers. You thought that your best friend was right if he or she did something different from what you were told not to do.

Overall, you seemed to have a knowing about life better than anyone else. We have all been there. Something happens to all of us when our curiosity is born. Our curiosity brings us once again closer to the one reality that all people want to experience. It is the triumph! So naturally we start turning over all those unturned pages, seeking to have new discoveries, and, needless to say, we avoid no location if we are serious about finding our own purpose in life. I think it is wise to ask other people about their experiences first in life, then, move forward with your own. Asking people to share their insight about the things that have happened in their lives can be very insightful.

All the while, keep in mind that you are

Ask, Seek, and Knock

part of everyone's life because in some way all that we have ever known has been a stockpile of all the memories of people having been here before us and people presently among us. I understand it to some degree. You and I must realize that the whole creation was created from a unity consciousness. Everything was made for everything and everybody to survive. All things are a type of trade off for all things.

All living things are part of one chain although there are insurmountable links. In the cycle of the triumph, all of us are here to discover what each other has to offer, and at the same time, all of us are to offer each other something different. There is only one way to find out what we individually offer each other without asking. I take it a step further. If I question my purpose in life, I can disassemble into parts my ignorance and locate the discovery of what I am to be and what I may share with others. I believe that this is the knowing handed over to me from the God voice in my higher consciousness. The Unity consciousness behind the creation designed life as a relay. Every person in each generation has a role to play and a baton to hold and pass on to the next person and/or generation.

Ask, Seek, and Knock

  When I was a boy, my great grandmother Addie Smith Johnson revealed this insight to me. Little did I know that I was being informed on how the secret principle of the unity consciousness designed my life. I will never lose focus of these words I was told by my great grandmother, "Son, everybody has a race to run." It did stick with me. She, at the age of ninety, finished her race but not without bringing me closer to the one reality of triumph. I thank God she helped me so much by answering all of my questions to the best of her ability. I was at the time living with her when God called me to preach Jesus' Gospel.

  You, like I, have so many great experiences to share. Truly, I believe that everyone has a book to be written and nobody's book is the same but everybody's book is in some way part of everyone's experience. It was said that there once lived a man revered as the wisest man to record experiences in his life time. I was told that he brought the whole creation closer to the triumph. It is said that the voice of God in higher consciousness revealed these words to him in a proverb, "As iron sharpens iron so does one man sharpen another." To me, this is one of the most important insights into the triumph.

Ask, Seek, and Knock

    Never are you to think that you do not need other people and their experiences. To do so, it becomes a setback to the entire progress of bringing ourselves to the triumph. I do believe that you are supposed to be in a position available for the whole creation to know your story. Everyone is as iron according to Solomon, this man whom I am referencing in the above-mentioned quotation. We all are capable of helping each other reach our fullest human height-triumph.

    Asking, seeking, and knocking are the terminology of Jesus Christ the redeemer of the triumph. I believe that the whole creation has been rescued with the insight of the triumph of Jesus Christ. His words, "Ask, and it shall be given you; seek, and ye shall find; knock it shall be opened unto you; for everyone that asks receives, and he that seeks finds; and to him that knocks, it shall be opened." To me, this wisdom offers several keys to the triumph. First, getting closer than you are to the triumph is what these words embrace. All things hold a type of mystery. I like to believe that every mystery can be revealed but not until after it is brought into question. *Ask* is

Ask, Seek, and Knock

another word for *question*. I know that questioning that which you do not know gets it to release its insight or mystery. The brilliance of your life is measured by the answers that you have found out by questioning the purpose of your life. Ask and it shall be given you! In the process of receiving the unborn insight for which you are waiting, several things happen. Initially, you open yourself up to a state of nothingness, and, therefore, inspired insight creates meaning in the way that you put yourself into what you are seeking. Then, as a seeker of what you are attempting to release, you become it for a split second consciously; thus, the voice of God coming out of a higher level of consciousness gives over the insight of mystery so that you understand it through becoming it, thus, knocking until the door comes open.

After I had been given this awareness via God in a shift of consciousness, to my discovery, God had decided to use me to bring myself closer to the triumph. Almost every time in your life, should you need to disassemble ignorance of things that you do not know, you will find out that you are not waiting for it to surface. Instead, becoming closer to what you want awaits you to

Ask, Seek, and Knock

go beyond the surface of your skin to retrieve it.

The whole idea of the one reality of the triumph is to observe all things as if you are all and all are in you. I believe this is how Jesus, the Master Teacher and others like unto Him possessed knowing all. At least, it is the way that I connect with all to possess all there is to know about all there is to see. The asking, seeking and knocking terminology used by Jesus Christ was the premise to be acknowledged in order to perform miracles. I have to believe it because it is the same way that I have. One simple way to define a miracle is to see it as a shift in consciousness. In other words, learn to observe mistakes in consciousness; therefore, you will know how to shift into a higher state of consciousness unborn.

The key is to observe it to perfect it. Through keen observation, insight of the mysterious is released and nothing can hide from diligent observation. When one asks for it, seeks, it and knocks on its door without ceasing, miracles are not hard to perform. Miracles are the result of carefully observing conscious shifts in the way that you direct your attention to become aware of mistakes in consciousness.

This is the way that I describe it. The

Ask, Seek, and Knock

triumph is all about erasing mental and spiritual mistakes. Believe me, all of us are wrapped very tight with those mistakes until the triumph brings us out of them. The triumph suggests that all people were created from the same consciousness, and, therefore, all things hold the mystery of God. By this, I mean, all things are the meaning of God, and you can see God's work in all things, especially within your consciousness.

    One day I got up out of bed only to discover the truth about where God placed wisdom, and, to my finding, I realized that it had come to me several times before I thought about where it may be hid. I was observing some very heavy questions about why some people, including myself, at season in my life, felt like we missed God in terms of our decision and/or choices. These decisions and choices placed us in conditions leading to more questions about where we had gone wrong or come up short of the best opportunities that life can offer.

    I needed to know where to find wisdom because within it lay many instructions which would manifest the triumph. I quickly received an awareness, a type of knowing about where to find wisdom. I learned about 21 years

Ask, Seek, and Knock

ago where to find it. Wisdom is found in everything with which you interact. Wisdom is spread over life, in everything, everywhere, every person, every day, every experience, every relationship, every religion, every happening under the sun because God, too, is wisdom!

In some conscious way, the vastness of wisdom is as the vastness of God. The amount of wisdom one needs in life is the amount it requires to ask for what you do not know; therefore, your own personal triumph can be enhanced. The triumph is an engagement that no living soul can escape. So does the triumph accept your challenges to be put into question so that you may begin sooner than later to dismantle ignorance into parts and locate the discovery of what you are to become. It matters not how much time it takes for you to figure out that you are closer than you were minutes ago. What matters is that you are closer than you were minutes ago to manifesting the greatest convenience you can possess while you are living and dying daily which is a sense of peace.

Ask, Seek, and Knock

5

Defeating Your Demons

I can prevail against any disguise of myself no matter the imaginary foe that I have created as long as I am willing to recreate myself in the process erasing my fears.

     Triumph comes with a price. It is not so much the price of money, medicine, and time. Rather the triumph is the price of self-sacrifice. As is with any battle in your life that you may be engaged, the real ways to wage the war are always mental. It is just a notion to recreate yourself from all your inner foes. The idea that you are going to make adjustments in your mental capacity must start with erasing your fears about losing the battle. Mental and spiritual conflicts wage their war on the reality of your mindset. I

Defeating Your Demons

suggested to myself at the time I encountered what I termed to be a demon that I could not hand over my mind if I were to become the victor. In the triumph, the warfare for the mind mentally and spiritually is at stake. What I have determined with myself is that I am a person capable of inhabiting dual natures: on the one hand, a good decent nature and on the other hand, an evil, indecent nature.

Every person has these dual natures. Often one nature is more enticing than the other, while at the same time they are ever competing for first place in our minds. Thus, there is born within us conflict. Inner conflict has to be sorted out in order to defeat inward foes of the soul. The larger the character of either nature within us, the more the elements of that nature can create invisible forces to drive us away from the other. Over a period of time, this produces inner reverberation. At some point most of the people on the planet will face an inhuman forceful inner self which becomes their demon. Demons are to be dealt with from an inward shifting of your lesser nature being darkened to your higher nature being heightened. I would like to make this as simple as possible for you to understand your demon and/

Defeating Your Demons

or demons. For some, the term lesser inner voice being not so humane is characterized as a demon, but it matters not how we describe the inner confusion. What matters most is how to deal with it.

Many years ago, practices of Christian asceticism provided its followers an ideal spiritual process which started in the eastern world and was later embraced by the western world, and it brought the entire world closer to finding the one reality of the triumph to prevailed demons. In one single insight of the awareness of asceticism these words I believe can sum it and likely have saved many lives from defeat: *struggle with the demons is at the same time struggle with alignment of the inner self.* Defeating your demons insists that your mind has to make a choice one way or the other whom it will obey. In the triumph, I am inclined to believe that much of the awareness about prevailing over demons comes down to choosing which voice you are going to serve if there are voices, hunches, and spirits.

No matter the struggle with the demons, it will always be the battle for your obedience. For me, this is the way my eyes were opened to understanding and being enlightened so that I

Defeating Your Demons

could know the insight of the triumph and the exceeding revelation of its power to reign above principalities, powers, rulers of darkness of this world, and against spiritual wickedness in high places. From this point of view of knowing, the world in which I interact depends on me in terms of victory and defeat.

    Jesus Christ taught us that in the triumph, we have power over serpents and scorpions and over all the power of the enemy within the self. In the triumph, the experience with life, my awareness knows that the one to be overcome is at the same time the one needing to be recreated both mentally and spiritually, the self. The work of self is personal. No one can do it for anyone else. It is among the journeys that cannot be accompanied. Once you erase your fears about what can plague you and once you replace your reality with believing that you can mentally and spiritually recreate yourself, there will be nothing to prevail against you. Holding on to memories that are not productive slows you down from mental and spiritual renewal.

    Over twelve years ago, I received an abundant insight on the power of belief. The term belief defines what one holds to be true and self

Defeating Your Demons

evident according to him or me. I have to see it this way because only what I believe actually comes alive within me. Defeating your demons takes up a greater percentage of inner power than anything else. When conquering your demons, just know that most of the work is mind control. The other part of the work is imaginative. I do agree that there are imaginary foes created in the mind. Your imagination can create anything. It's a type of formless creative tool given to you to help you create and recreate. Defeating your demons is partly imaginary as well. The knowledge of your imagination holds all the mysteries of your inner foes.

All demons play to the fear of your heart. Just about all the issues of your life are in your heart, and your dual natures compete for your mind control and, therefore, race to your heart for your attention. I believe that when you accept the understanding of the dual natures to be there as balancers instead of warriors one against the other, you learn to appreciate both of them for what they can do for each other in terms of balance. Mental and spiritual balance destroys your demons. In the grand scheme of things a demonic activity is the reflection of your mind out

Defeating Your Demons

of control.

    This is likely because the mind at the time is imbalanced. Likely, the lesser of your dual natures is imbalanced; however, when the purest of your dual natures balances the lesser nature, balance is the impact. Once this happens the struggle collapses for mind control and therefore, calm inhabits your mind. In the triumph, only balance is seen as the tool to collapse inner conflict so that only calm and/or peace are born. The work of destroying your demons is the process of sorting out and cleaning up imbalanced thoughts so that you balance the different types of inner conflict, learned behavior, restricted tendencies and torment due to some form of captivity lingering in your thinking pattern.

    The only certainty of resolving anything about you is to deal with it mentally. The key is getting to know your inner self. Everything about you is your inner self. Even the world is within the inner self. Just think about it. God has set the world within man. This is true according to the wisest man noted in the Bible. Solomon is his name. He said, "God has set the world within a man's heart…." After questioning this verse in the Bible, I quickly realized that it was the same as

Defeating Your Demons

interpreting all things with the mind. By so doing, I came to know myself differently from what I had been taught about myself. Then, I understood that I was filtering every aspect of life within my heart and my mind. Thus, I was the giver of meaning to everything that was in my mind, even the co-creator of everything in my mind. I, therefore, realized the triumph of life and know it to be certain that I embrace everything with my mind and within my mind is everything that is, that was, that shall be, and that could be. Even the world is in me because it is in my mind. Today, I see myself as all things because all things are in my mind.

This means that I am getting closer to the triumph although I am not quite there. Seemingly, the triumph is ever creating new moments causing one to come closer to abstracting from the fear of being in a state of unity consciousness with God rather than being God. This is frightening to most people because most people think that they can never reach a state of God consciousness. I differ with most people on this subject. God has no problem with me being equal with Divine consciousness in contrast to being equal to Divine consciousness. I take this to mean that except we are transformed by the renewing

Defeating Your Demons

of our minds, we lack knowing all that we possess, and, if God is in our minds, we are at least Godly or Godlike.

How you see God is the question that will determine the quality of your mind. Your mind is capable of infinite power should you acknowledge that it is the spiritual form of God, and no foe can hide from it. God only wants you to know yourself: what you are and what you are not. I am certain I know myself, and this is good enough for me. In other words, I am just what I am. I will leave myself open to just being that I am until I choose to be something next.

Until you see yourself in this manner, you will always restrict yourself to your thoughts, other people's thoughts and perceptions of you, and eventually the product of someone's mind control. Never allow your mind to be controlled although it is everyone's wishes for you; it is every intention of the law; even every intention of your demons should you allow the existence of them. Pursue the triumph in that it releases brand new consciousness.

6

The Worst Evil

Should I not recognize that, disguises are subliminal and should I not recognize all attempts seeking to control my mind of freewill, evil prevents me from seeing my inner self.

The moment I thought about providing a personal explanation of what I had experienced as the worst evil imaginable I wanted to be sure that I would be fair on observing the topic of evil. I thought many times, "What if I had not encountered every evil." So I had to approach evil differently. Then, I realized that I needed to delve as deep as I could into what defines evil before I could handle the terms "worst evil." Immediately my imagination, sparked by curiosity, so carefully delved into evil in the surest way possible to

The Worst Evil

understand it. For a split second, as I attempted to define evil, I imagined it being a type of unconscious state within myself causing ruin, injury, or pain.

All of a sudden, I realized that only my heart and mind could cause me the worst ruin, injury, or pain; therefore, the worst evil had to be the subtle disguised manipulation of one's heart and mind. Quickly, I found my answer to evil. Wherever there is any form of disguised control of one's mind and/or by any means to cause manipulation or control of it, the worst evil is being performed in it. The worst evil controls from an unconscious state of having freewill to exercise individuality. Increasingly, many people are finding out that once they free themselves from the opinion or influence of all of the incoming minds in their circle of rapport, they are freed from the emotions, feelings, self injury, and pain associated with obeying other people's expectations which rendered them blameworthy any way. I have this personal belief about myself. My soul yearns to be free at all times, so should I allow my inner self to live in a state of unconsciousness to the insurmountable freedoms? If so, I am allowing my inner self to

The Worst Evil

abide in a state of unconscious death.

That which you allow to manipulate your mind causes harm, misfortune, or destruction because you have been trained to walk in the authority of mental insecurity rather than being directed by an unrestricted conscious. I suggest then the worst evil blinds the mind of its real enemy being an unconscious state and its being the source from which you are identifying your life. God has taught me that the *triumph is an adventure that enlightens the mind, soul, and spirit.*

During the time I was preparing this chapter, I thought about how often all of us have blamed everybody or every kind of situation, condition, and crisis for the reason we were being victimized. The real victimization is the way that you were trained to think about those things in your life because of the way your mind has been programmed when all the while the blame has been the subtle disguise of your mind being manipulated by what you term to be your blame. It has always been mind deception that renders you the worst ruin, pain, deception, and injury. The fact that you have need to blame anything other than the mind's deception has been

The Worst Evil

because evil disguises itself so that you don't see the real enemy being once your mind misaligned.

What is more, your mind is giving meaning and defining your reality. Therefore, if it has not all the liberty and freedom to envision beyond what has been laid out for you to believe, the mind is deprived and it will create what you call problems. In my quest of the triumph, I found an insight so radical that it shifted my consciousness so that evil could no longer lie hidden.

What I discovered is that when my mind was free to create any meaning instead of the meaning of life given to me to believe, I recreated my reality of myself, the world, people, and providence. Until you are free to recreate yourself via inner adjustments, you don't know how to take yourself to a next dimension. During my adventure to find the worst evil, I found it to be sublime, underneath my eyes keeping me from recognizing that it was the function of my being. This awareness recovered me with the understanding that my mind should only be given the liberty to be equal with God. There is a vast difference between its being equal with God and equal to God.

There is a profound inspiration in the Bible

The Worst Evil

that brought me closer to the triumph shared in these words by the Apostle Paul. "Let this mind be in you which was first in Christ Jesus who thought it not robbery to be equal with God but take upon yourself to be in the form of God's servant and humble yourself..." found in Philippians 2: 5-8. This inspiration is so empowering because it suggests knowing that your mind is capable of being equal with the ultimate reality that governs all life.

I have come to believe that when your mind has the wrong focus governing it, the evil that you cannot and do not recognize is the misalignment with ultimate consciousness because at such time, infinite consciousness has been that which eludes you. There is a shift in consciousness that occurs during the triumph over the worst evil being mind deficient.

Let's examine some of the changes that take place during the triumph. To begin, engaging in the flow of the triumph, your imagination exceeds your mind with a greater awareness which your soul expresses. In the expression, free will, intuition and inspiration find their way back to your original self, being potentiality and possibility. The brilliance of the return to your

The Worst Evil

triumph is to know that you posses all and not be tempted to be all because you know that all is in you and flows through you.

Instead, allow yourself to live with knowing that you were born to remain possibility and potentiality until you are ready to fulfill some greater cause which could bring the entire world again closer to the triumph: the ultimate reality. I am here to inform all of us that taking ourselves to the next dimension above mental insecurity is the purpose of the triumph. Let's be not deceived. Reaching the triumph will take sacrifice and concentration which will result in conflict of interest to accepting your normal learned behavior. In the process of the triumph, you will define your purpose to be total awareness.

Your goal becomes reaching an understanding that can recover your mind, the authority of your life from anyone else's thoughts, perception, feelings and memory of life. You, therefore, experience a new life born, one each day that you use your new mind. There was a certain man who lived many years ago that many Christians read about even until this day who said, "Be not conformed to this world but be transformed by the renewing of your mind that

The Worst Evil

you may prove what is acceptable...." To me, what an insight this man had thousands of years ago for the same purpose about which I am speaking to you in the pages of this book, which is to help you become closer to a new reality of yourself.

The reason a new reality is so vital from your mind being locked outside of reconciliation is because everything reflects your interpretation because you create your own interpretation. I know this to be true. The world is within your heart because your heart embraces the world according to its feelings about the world.

Until you learn how to separate the world from your heart to seeing it as a view in your consciousness, you come short of overcoming the world. The way of the triumph is to overcome the world as you see the world being within you and not you in the world, but that the world is not what you see. The world is viewed in your consciousness. I once questioned this awareness myself until I read the Bible. There are two places within the Bible that opened awareness to this insight that you may find intriguing.

In my search for higher meaning of the world, during my theological studies, I located in the poetic books in the Bible the wisdom that

The Worst Evil

helped the entire creation see a once fleeting reality of the world. Examine these words and see if you can see what I have said already about the position of the world: "God has set the world within man so that he could not find out beginnings…." Ecclesiastes 3:11.

I believe God set the world within you because the last place that you would seek God is within your inner self. There are many reasons to believe that God made man wonderfully, and this can be proven. The consciousness of human being is creative, and the road to the triumph reunites you to that creativity. In other words, there is no way to prove the world except by the way you wrap your heart and mind around it with emotions coming from your interpretation being an inner power. This is the recovery that the self takes on in the triumph.

Having said that, the entire interpretation of the world is created by human beings and passed along in some form or another to all the lesser creatures. You are not the world, the world is within you. The fact is that the world does not exist without a consciousness to interpret or behold it. This is mentally and spiritually speaking!

The Worst Evil

The worst evil being recovered is the renewal of your orientation of thinking with an emphasis placed on the replacement of the world viewed in your conscious rather than outside of it. You are what you perceive for that matter. "For as a man thinks in his heart so is he" are words from the greatest wisdom ever---King Solomon. The point here is supporting the fact that the world is supported by your thoughts and interpretation. In the triumph, one's emphasis is to shift his or her thoughts from an outer to an inner state or next dimension.

I am here to tell you that your triumph suggests that you think like God without any limitation. Limitation is part of the circle of evil. The mind of God is the mind that thinks the way no man has ever thought! Now, this is how to transform oneself from the worst evil. Just think! A brand new thought, one that has not ever been given to anyone before you is the beginning of new creation. I qualify that any brand of new thought brought into the mind of man, if never any other man has thought, becomes a miracle because it forms new creative ingenuity into the material state when acted on.

The Worst Evil

You will discover that in the triumph, the brand new energy that you acquire is the main ingredient of taking yourself to a next dimension. Brand new thoughts always bring brand new responses into the world. Not to mention, brand new thoughts bring brand new actions into the world. So now, you tell me if the world that you once knew as totally physical is not a production of the thought and/or conscious behind it. The world is both God's and yours, and you, too, are both yourself and the lesser self of God!

I thought about something just recently. Maybe you have, too, at least once. What if I gave myself an opportunity to recreate my inner self? What if I opened my consciousness to see things as I have not ever seen them, my mind to do things unborn, and my ears to listen to the inner rhythm of creativity? That is what I am calling triumph. The thought which no mind has ever conceptualized inspires you to be more creative. Thus, you can be the newest creation, and old things can pass and no longer be part of your memory. As you come closer to your triumph, you will remember that victory over the worst evil is to be viewed through identifying it as inward rather than outward and that the victory of life

The Worst Evil

over death is inner identification. Products of your identity seemingly are things that you create in life, and how you value those creations defines how you give meaning and value to life. Your inner self is the reflection of your identity here and hereafter.

7

You Don't Have To Fear Evil

Evil is the course to expose me to me and bigger and better things as I uncover it to be the beginning of triumph.

All of my life, I have watched people run in the opposite direction of triumph. They are afraid to face evil. I was taught to do the same thing until one day I noticed something very rewarding about facing evil. Evil poses as a big bully, but it is as precious as a friend. For most people, they would see this reality as distant from east to west, but when you observe evil closely, you will discover that it releases the knowledge of the triumph.

When you learn not to accept that evil is designed to cause harm, misfortune, or

You Don't Have To Fear Evil

destruction, as you have been taught, there is something missing or left out from evil. What is left out of evil is the knowledge of correction and wisdom. Surely, no one enjoys making the same mistakes that render oneself repeated harm, misfortune, or destruction. Therefore, the evil that you encounter from yourself and/or others during times of interacting with it causes you to seek God.

It is as if all things are working their way back to good after a few encounters with evil. I am sure that evil has its role to play in your personal triumph. I, therefore, say that you don't have to be afraid of evil. The opposite of evil is good; thus, after you have accepted evil as an introductory course to good, you can learn to appreciate it as your stepping stone to bigger and better things.

I wanted so badly to see evil as my enemy, as do most people, but in my triumph I have learned to view it as a reason to change what I have termed to be the reason for my misfortune. I have learned on the journey to triumph that evil brought me closer to my personal awareness of how to involve myself with good or, as I call it, bigger and better things.

You Don't Have To Fear Evil

Taking a closer look at evil, I would have to say that it has a type of involvement with every person, and there is really no way around it. It does not matter who you are, what church you attend, and or what you profess to be. Its involvement serves as an instructor leading you away from misfortune, ruin, destruction, and defeat. I believe there is a single insight to be gotten from my involvement with the misfortune caused by evil.

It subliminally says you must first crawl before you can walk. So I am here to tell you that you want to walk away from ignorance. This is one of the best things anyone can accomplish. You do not have to fear evil because you gain wisdom through experiencing it. You, therefore, learn how to make adjustments in your mind and memory. Have you ever noticed your growth after your experience with evil is over? Yep, you grow from your experience with it.

I have been told always from my youth up that you learn from your mistakes, and this is the way that I view evil. Just another mistake from which to grow is a valid interpretation of evil in your life. Once you begin to grow, you overcome the presence of evil in your life. Several

You Don't Have To Fear Evil

occurrences happen during the growth process. Let us view those things. For now, we will just call them growing pains. After evil has been faced internally or has been a lesson in your mind in which your mind is a view in consciousness, you tend to demonstrate good morality.

Equally important, your awareness develops a type of maturity in a gradual process. At some point, after some rounds with evil, we learn to deal with it from the position of a series of events that we have lived through; thus, we are no longer afraid of it because we have experienced it before. Evil is always typically repeating itself until one learns to move beyond it. In the triumph, evil is seen for what it really is, misfortune. Evil always reveals the guilt of wrong doing and misfortune. It will bring you closer to the triumph should you learn to see evil and face it as an education to bring you to your triumph. This is the way God planned it.

If new gain in your life is to come, you will need to know how to overcome evil encountered and not react in fear and weakness. The adventure that I am terming as triumph awaits you! Take it. Don't fear it. You no longer have to fear evil. Face it and be the victor. The Bible

You Don't Have To Fear Evil

teaches that you are more than a conqueror through the strength of God. For this matter, it is what any spiritual leader teaches or should teach you. If not, you are not taking steps toward the triumph.

RESIST NOT EVIL –Jesus Christ St. Matthew 5:39. I might suggest to you, go beyond it!

You Don't Have To Fear Evil

All things work together. Good and evil do also. Good is the awakening from evil and evil is the dark side of good. They are one reality with two extremes!

8

What Plays to My Heart Breaking

I am able to observe where I make mistakes with focus and not lose sight of existing disguises; therefore, I do always know my desires.

 One of the most subtle things to be dealt with during the time of your triumph is the position your heart takes on issues pertaining to outcomes. For a long time, I never questioned my heart's position about certain issues in my life. I have learned that it's necessary to observe my heart's position if I am to govern my heart instead of my heart's governing me with all of its wants. It is vital that at some point you take control over what you allow to exist in your heart. By so doing,

What Plays to My Heart Breaking

you are in the best possible position for triumph.

There is a paradoxical biblical saying, *"Keep thy heart diligent. For in it are the issues of life."* I do see how God used this insight to sew up all the gaps once opened by our hearts' craving everything in the path of our eyes. This insight of King Solomon can bring us closer to what plays to the wants of our hearts. The heart is the critical issue in our lives because it wraps its feelings around anything that we put in it; thus, it never wants to let them go. Everything that you put in your heart creates desire.

The moment that you allow desire to set in your heart it longs and request for permanence. This means that whatever you allow your heart to embrace, the more your heart does not expect for you to change it. This can be a setback to triumph.

The above-mentioned paradoxical insight suggests that you watch with diligence what you allow to exist in your heart because of the position in which your heart will put you about removing it. The heart's feelings do not turn loose easy; so you need to watch what you allow to exist in your heart. Your very life is within your heart! Do not take it lightly. Wants in your heart can lead to addiction, and if unfulfilled, those

What Plays to My Heart Breaking

wants will make you suffer. In the triumph, your heart becomes the issue that has to be dealt with before any real awareness can come to rescue you from hurt. The triumph has shown me that my heart is very desirous. Again, it must be kept! It wants all things so that it can experience feelings for all things. I have discovered that the more you submit to its wants, the more it wants. The more wants it gets, the more it doesn't want to release.

It sets up conquests for inner conflict when you start to dismiss its cravings. Literally, it works against you, and your mind knows what it must do to replace those wants that are not good for you to hold inside. The fact of life is that it is in a constant change which cannot be reversed; therefore, your heart has to be tamed, not your mind. Your heart, if not tamed, is what plays to your hurt, pain, and destruction! It will hinder you from moving forward with the changes that come in your life which are not reversible.

Thus, your heart will cause you to suffer want. I have noticed that wants unfulfilled cause withdrawal, suffering, and grievance, all of which attack your happy state. The triumph leads you closer to another form of happiness after you have tamed your heart with diligence. The new

What Plays to My Heart Breaking

awareness that comes with monitoring your heart is discipline. Discipline, therefore, protects your heart from the ruin of want and/or desire. One of the rewards of your triumph will prove to be divine character and behavior resulting from training your heart to have the authority of self control. Discipline produces moral and mental improvement which is the whole matter of the triumph. If your heart is not subjected to discipline, it may lead to one's ruin, falling short of the triumph. Recently, I was given an insight about how to deal with the heart in terms of its adapting to change, and I was not surprised that it had to undergo a gradual process of abstinence. Needless to say, I was not surprised because I had read many books about how to discipline my flesh, but the Bible introduced fasting to me. I do believe the two concepts abstinence and fasting are similar.

Once, I read a story about how self control empowered the self. Only by achieving self control, there come miraculous abilities to the one possessing it. There are two things that you must know about yourself before triumph comes. On the one hand, you will need to be able to observe your mistakes. All mistakes result from

What Plays to My Heart Breaking

issues in your heart. Once you are able to observe yourself, you are also able to repair yourself without going to others seeking counsel except that of God.

Very few people want to see their flaws. I suggest that everyone knows his or her flaws. Else, how can you heal your heart with your mind? On the other hand, you need to stay focused on what enters your heart. There must be a lifelong diligence to observe the interests of your heart. With this in mind, there is one subtle foe left to contend with for the heart. It's called disguise. Disguise is the hardest thing for your heart to detect because it conceals its appearance. Be encouraged because nothing can really escape the diligence of careful observation although it is subtle. In my own personal life, disguise once played to the desires of my heart; therefore, I was kept blind to my inner self as the real source of my cravings.

Unless there is diligence to observe it, you will never focus on the real issue to blame. Disguised desire is hardest to find because it takes you away from seeing yourself craving for wants as needs when really wants and needs are two different issues altogether. What is more, the

What Plays to My Heart Breaking

work of sorting through wants and needs is the lifelong project should one never bring his or her heart to discipline of wants. In the big picture a want is classified as a request. When requests are followed without some previous investigation, it can be just wishful thinking; whereas, a need is characterized as pending its existence. There are so many things that we qualify as needs when really they are part of a habitual cycle of wishful thinking, very hard to detect. Most helpful to me during certain triumph in my life, was the insight of discernment. All deception of your heart is part of the cycle of wishful thinking. Wishful thinking can do so many things to you. Just look at how many times you were disappointed by wishful thinking which renders you disappointed because your want was not supplied.

9

Emotions the Big Conflict

Emotions keep people either holding on or letting go. Emotions don't remain constant. They are always in a state of fluctuation.

    Nothing affects every aspect of your life as do your emotions. You may be wondering if your emotions cause you both the best and worst time in your life. The answer is without a doubt, yes! Reason being, your emotions are the part of consciousness that involves feelings. They have direct influence on you. In most cases your emotions come with consequences. There is an outcome associated with our lives that has much to do with our emotions. Learning how to control your emotions seems to be your big conflict. In the triumph, you discover the simple

Emotions the Big Conflict

truth about your emotions. They are identifiers that reveal how you are identifying with every meaning of your life.

    My personal triumph suggested to me to define life. When I did, I discovered my emotions. Some of them were twisted, others of them were weird, many of them were misaligned with learned behavior, majority of them needed to be treated with tender hands, a number of them were fragile, and very few of them were rewarding to me except those that were pleasurable. My quest deeper into the meaning of my life pointed me to inner identity which my emotions were either in front of my identification of life or at least impulses with which my life responded. The question that you will have to answer for yourself during your triumph is "What reveals my emotions?" For me, I discovered that my perception revealed my emotions; therefore, my emotions were the reflection of the reality of my perception. When one first finds where emotions are seated, one gains deeper insight of his or her triumph.

    This key victory to understanding yourself helps you to recover yourself from wounds created by your emotions. One of the very closest

What Plays to My Heart Breaking

insights of the triumph is perception. I would like for you to use the word *my view* for perception. It is your view on life that does always birth your emotions. In addition, your view and/or outlook on life is your reality. Reality is not so hard to change. I had to realize during my triumph that reality escalates and that I could change my emotions.

The process of elimination of painful emotions was just a matter of learning what to do to change my emotions. This year alone, I had the strongest awareness come to me about changing my emotional state of being. God allowed me to see myself for what I had become because of my emotions. And the only way to reposition was to seek a higher identification of myself if I was going to ever sever emotions that revealed both the best and worst of me. You will probably agree that our emotions control our actions. If anyone wants to change his or her action, he or she must know how to change his or her emotional state. Emotions, if not properly aligned with a perception of none interference with the actions and reactions of others, can cause consequences with which you would never agree. Did you know that emotions cause people to do what they do? It

What Plays to My Heart Breaking

is not wise to play with emotions. I advise anyone to take emotions seriously.

Emotions are impulsive. In the search for strength, you have to deal with emotions. Emotions can either make or break you, help or hurt, and the work of facing your emotions can be called self help if you can be honest with yourself. It is one of the hardest challenges in life, also the most rewarding in life. I had to observe my emotions with every aspect of my life to find my discovery of triumph. Looking at my emotions, I first fainted. Afterwards, the work was inescapable. To my discovery, emotions and my morality had to be worked out. To the degree of perfection, my perception being the place where emotions originated, I had to reach a non-opinionated and non-interfering position for there to be a quality of self improvement to occur within me. It is necessary to understand this insight into the triumph should you be honest about repositioning your emotions. I had to realize that in the grand scheme of morality that my emotions were subtle and, therefore, could not be overlooked.

Emotions are tied to spirituality. For me, I describe spirituality as four tenants: imagination,

What Plays to My Heart Breaking

belief, intention and awareness. Emotions run higher in spirituality than any other aspect, likely, because they are spread over these four tenants all in one. If you pay attention to emotional states from a religious point of view, cultures have been taken by the hand of emotions and in many ways remain victims of emotions swallowed up by the forces of emotions.

The distance between strength and weakness can be closed when you become conscious enough to understand that your reactions of spirituality are subject to your feelings about what you believe. I know that the big question that you have for me now is, "Where does God fit in with my emotions?"

I can only speak with God in mind rather than speak for God. Whereas, your emotions are part of your conscious, God's Spirit is the makeup of your consciousness! The Spirit of God in your emotions is best in terms of well being! With God in mind, there can be no conflict and, therefore, emotions, the big conflict, can be transformed by the renewal of your perception. The triumph of my life suggested that I love God more than anything else and softened my emotions about everything else. How you interpret God and the

What Plays to My Heart Breaking

meaning of your life will help you resolve your emotions about what happens in your life and the lives of your loved ones.

It is necessary to give careful observation to your emotions so that you can get a grip on life in terms of what you should be holding onto and/or letting go. This process of elimination can help you take on new meaning in your life, and a new life can be the result of your emotions being repaired and/or restructured. So many times in my life I have had to revisit my emotions so that I could keep my feelings from running out of my control. Chances are that you, too, have witnessed your emotions taking you beyond your restraints.

Don't feel bad because everyone has to deal with this conflict before the triumph can come. Hopefully, now you have gained some clarity about yourself in the way that you can improve as you recreate your emotions about yourself as well as others. I would like to encourage you never to fear facing your emotions because that is the only way to know yourself and redesign yourself.

Every human being desires to redesign certain things about self. The way is made. Problem being, some people, places and things in

What Plays to My Heart Breaking

your life will be replaced at the same time that you confront your emotions about what can or cannot stay. I know.

It is painful to reposition memories of your past because of relationships being inclusive. There is a little known saying that seems to fit into your life at this point in the triumph, *no pain no gain!* For a long time, I failed to observe this saying when I had to reposition my life from certain emotions. At the time all that I could feel was pain; however, through pain I gained the strength to either let go or hold on. In most cases, I gained awareness about myself so that I could give myself another peaceful moment.

Peace is probably the greatest achievement of the triumph. Now, what all people must ask themselves when dealing with the conflict of their emotions in terms of putting them in order is *"How much do I value peace of mind?"* The work of dealing with your emotions is all about gaining peace with yourself, peace with everyone else, and peace in God. When you love peace enough, your emotions won't be a conflict anymore for you to put in perspective; therefore, the triumph is inevitable.

10

Subliminal Seduction

Beneath the very surface of my eyes, there are some things worth finding out. Should I, I am a step ahead. Should I not, I am left in the dark!

I have often wondered if life could be any better for me during times that I was in poverty, sick, helpless, without money, and being down and out of touch with how people make millions of dollars. From time to time I would sit and think about why I was unfortunate and so many others were fortunate. I wonder sometimes if it was meant for me to have abundance in life. Maybe, this has not been your experience, but the triumph suggests that abundance is available to me if I want it in my life. I had to find out what was keeping me from abundance. Often, I would

Subliminal Seduction

blame myself.

    I soon discovered that blaming myself for coming up short of other people's expectation was not the cause of my lack of well being. Instead, it was my inability to see what lay beneath the surface of my eyes that kept me on the opposite side of abundance. It was subliminal seductions away from proper consciousness that closed my eyes to my mistakes in consciousness which rendered me poor, sickly, helpless, without money, etc. The triumph reveals that subliminal seduction as leading one away from self examination leaves oneself locked outside of revelation to abundance.

    Without the proper awareness of your own capacity to change your life by recognizing certain mistakes in your consciousness, the role of the inner self becomes obsolete. What does this mean? It means that deeply within your consciousness, accountability is given to you. You are responsible for observing your own abundance, and there is no one to blame but you. Observation is an old practice but fits into every generation. The Bible and other spiritual books use the word meditation for observation or self examination. Regardless, of the terminology, the

Subliminal Seduction

practice of meditation aids you to journey back to yourself to see what is beneath the surface of your physical eyes. I don't know who coined the practice that self examination is the surest method to crush subliminal seductions, but I do know that everyone must examine himself or herself closely in order to come closer to the triumph. When you introspectively analyze your errors in consciousness, you gain awareness on how to realign yourself with abundant consciousness that shifts your outlook around and assists you with new insights to produce new outcomes in your life.

The subliminal seduction away from abundance becomes void. In the triumph to divine consciousness, there are some challenges to going ahead of previous states of your being. One of the challenges is the battle for the mind. Everything battles for the mind. It is not just one thought, instead all thoughts. The battle for the mind has to be dealt with by new awareness.

Many times in my life, I have had to reposition my mind from negative thoughts, negative predictions, negativity in general so that I could refocus on a higher state of awareness to get me out of what I was in during such times that

Subliminal Seduction

I felt defeated. Within the higher states of consciousness, I was able to defeat my previous mind which created my existing problem. Let me tell you. It worked! One of the last places to look to find knowledge of the triumph was within. It is also the place where I met my God.

Equally important to the two natures good and evil within us are two hunches that come to dictate them. Let's just call the two hunches pure and corrupt. Hunches within are impulses that are very dictating until you slow down to analyze them. Believe me, those things beneath the surface of your comprehension are worth knowing. Knowledge about your capacity as a human being can support you in so many beneficial ways. Also, a lack of knowledge can cripple you in so many ways.

The goal in the triumph is to slow your mind down in order to observe what you blame so that you can see that the real blame as mistakes in consciousness, and, therefore, a shift in your consciousness is all that you need to regain vitality and regain acceleration to discovering your own personal abundance. When you blame anything other than a shift in your consciousness, it makes you a subject of subliminal seduction to your inner

Subliminal Seduction

power. The inner power you need has always been there with you waiting to be employed. Just about all things in your life are the product of your conceptualizations.

The oldest case of subliminal seduction is biblical. It is the first story in the Bible. Adam and Eve were a couple. They were asked not to eat a certain forbidden fruit. Initially, Adam was obedient. Eve was curious about the fruit. It is said that she was enticed by her inner impulse after Satan's lecture about the wellness that the fruit would bring. Eve's impulse suggested that she eat; therefore, she became desirous to eat the forbidden fruit. The rest is history. They did eat. God was upset because of their sins. Then, Eve blamed Satan and Adam blamed Eve.

Here is what happened. Satan's lecture was no gun to Eve's head. Satan may have presented an enticing, tempting lecture, but the choice remained Eve's and Adam's. What I believe really happened was the first case of subliminal seduction. Here is why. Eve gave in to her desire and then subliminally she accused Satan because of the enticement. Who's really to blame here in terms of disobedience? You may ask yourself as I did. Did Satan make Eve eat or was Eve a victim of

Subliminal Seduction

a specific kind of desire that caused her ruin? She had the choice not to eat. She elected to eat. Did Satan put the fruit in her mouth? Did Satan induce her into a sleep to feed her? No! She was either irresponsible or weak. You may say the same about Adam. The Bible does say that Adam said that Eve gave him the fruit to eat. But could Adam have rejected Eve's gift? I think that he could have if he wanted to logically speaking. I know he chose to eat for any number of reasons. The fact is that Adam chose to eat. His blame was not Eve. He was subliminally blinded by love. Love for his wife was his reason for the transgression. The whole point that I am conveying is that we must recognize that most mistakes are the result of a lack of shift in our consciousness.

    The whole basis of the triumph is to open our eyes so that we see what we have never seen before about ourselves in a type of self actualizing way. Sure there are so many other schools of thoughts about who is the blame for your shortcomings, but the most logical explanation is that you were distracted from your best consciousness, therefore, deceived by your desire or lack of abstinence. The insight of consciousness is the clarity of the first and last adventure of

Subliminal Seduction

triumph. It either brings you to triumph or separates you from triumph. My advice to anyone is, "Stop looking for God in all the wrong places!" God is present within you! I have come to believe since I was a youth in my ministry that people complicate God. Which is easier to say, "God is within me and I in God" or "God is outside of me and I am without God in my life"?

God can open my eyes to what escapes my view on the surface. The triumph is God's knowledge released from the position of inner awakenings. I believe this is the very beginning of human evolution. I am not excluding the works of God in the physical realm; however, I am including God to be unrestricted in all realms, including you!

11

The Instructor That Never Leaves You

When you are ready to learn about yourself, all that you have experienced will be there to instruct you.

Haven't you ever wondered sometimes why you have to go through lessons or experiences in order to gain certain knowledge? I have come to understand that life is designed that way. Every breath we take in every moment is an experience, and in that experience we are interacting with breathing, which is a very important lesson should we want to continue to live.

Recently, I was fortunate to find out an insight about my life that no one ever told me. I

The Instructor That Never Leaves You

discovered that as long as I live, my breath was instructing me to breathe in and out. I perceived it to be the instructor that resides within me. Really that insight was not mind blowing until I viewed other instructors that never leave me. The triumph allowed me to see that as my breath was instructing me to breathe, so were my experiences instructing me to grow.

Experiences will always be part of living. There is really no way around experiencing life except you have no life. Experience is the instructor that assists you along the triumph. As long as you are in the world, you will be assisted by the wisdom of your experiences. Experiencing yourself is the lesson of the triumph because every aspect of your life is a reflection of yourself interacting with everything that you allowed to live within you.

It may be easier for me to tell you that your life is an experience which would be true; however, it is more actualizing to say to you that nothing can experience you until you give it permission no matter how it may be described. Reason being, an experience can only be an event or a series of events participated in or lived through you! The entire creation lives through all

The Instructor That Never Leaves You

of us. We are it, and it is we. The role of an instructor is to impart unto you, with assurance, knowledge, and hope to prepare you for a particular moment. You tell me, what other than experience does it any better for you.

Your instructor that never leaves you, therefore, is experience. So many beautiful outcomes are born out from your experiences with events through which you have previously lived. We access hope, patience, and peace from our experiences. The more of them you have had the greater the range of your wisdom. Your life is just like a movie with so many characters with various assignments.

The big picture is that each of the characters has assignments to give you, and at the end of the movie it will be your experience. In a very real way, people are in the blind if they have no experience with certain knowledge in life. I one day realized the value of experience after filling out many applications for jobs, credit, and opportunity. No one wants to give you a chance to prove what you are capable of unless most of the time you have had some experience with what you are applying yourself to do. After a while, all people learn to appreciate their experiences when

The Instructor That Never Leaves You

they have come through them. I do! Besides experience, all of the other instructors in your life are temporary.

They have a role to fulfill, then they fall into the vast part of experience for you. Have you ever thought about what you would be without experiences? I have. I would be void. I would be blind to reality. I would simply be crippled by not having experienced some lessons in life. What is most helpful for any person is experience!

Until you see what it can provide you, there it lies between you and truth, you and enlightenment, and you and fortune. I don't think that you can separate from experiences while living because your life is an experience in the now and beyond now. Everything that we enjoy about life is because we are able to experience it. If we were not able to experience the things in which we are engaged, we would not have any knowledge about the things that we know. Another word that I would like for you to think about when it comes to experiences is *habitable.* For sure if one wants to enjoy anything here on earth, take away experiencing it and discover there is nothing to enjoy.

There are some things that we all want to

The Instructor That Never Leaves You

leave us alone in this life. What is more, there are certain seasons that we want to end sooner than others, and there are some seasons that we want never to end. The triumph teaches you not to separate them, instead see them as education. There is certain education that no one can teach you except your life's experience; therefore, it is necessary that you go through all the lessons that make up your life.

With experience comes discernment. Believe me, you will need it in this life. Without discernment, all sorts of costly mistakes and setback are certain. In order for you to move your life ahead of each breathing moment, especially when you are not happy where you are, discernment as a result of your previous experience gives you intellect to perceive mentally your next move. Your experiences in life teach you how to make good judgment or perceptibility.

For me, I learned that my experience at a very youthful stage was creating my perspective. When you really look at your perspective, your previous experiences really play the greater part. It is your outlook that is split half during the triumph so that you project changes in life sufficient with your very own keenness about

The Instructor That Never Leaves You

ultimate reality. To add a thought, the triumph is designed to get you to observe experiences in your life as if they are necessary so that you see them not as challenges but compliments.

On the way to triumph, one discovers appreciation for all that he or she has come through. Ultimately, one looks back and views every experience as a tutor to bring about the victory of peace and triumph. Looking back over your experiences teaches you how to appreciate the present. Total deception is for you to learn nothing from life's experiences. Can you imagine yourself in a worse predicament should you not have gained some wisdom, education, and/or experience going through the trials and tribulations that are in your past?

I can answer that question for myself. I would be as lost as I could be. In the final analysis, your experiences are always with you to help you mature. You are the student and your experiences are the instructors. We are all in school so to speak. Everyday our experiences in life are training us. It would be wise to pay strict attention to the education of your experiences because they are helpers. The instructor that never leaves you is there to contribute to your happiness here,

The Instructor That Never Leaves You

to relieve you of doubt, and to improve the way that you go about doing things.

What else could your experiences be other than triumph! Every experience that you have had is useful to the whole creation because it is releasing an insight of advancement for human being. You are the piece of the puzzle that the whole creation has been waiting for in terms of sharing your insight. Even if your experience with a certain moment in your life was horrifying, it still is beneficial to someone somewhere. All people are benefiting from one another, and I believe that this is the way that God has planned for the triumph to come to all of us.

One of the commandments of God penned by Moses, the man of God, is "Do unto others as you would have them do unto you." This was an insight about creation, and there is only one greater than it, "Love God with all you heart." As you go along life, it is your duty to share with others what you have to contribute from your experiences so that others may share with you theirs, and all can benefit.

We are placed on the earth not to be self-centered; rather we are here to be united. Our common experiences create among us a bond

The Instructor That Never Leaves You

that also unites us. So if you had little or no experiences, you could not bond with other people that are around you. Experiences are bonding! They bring people together from all over the world. If you were really serious about thinking about what your experiences have done for you, you would never underestimate the benefit of your lifelong journey here on earth. Just remember, if you are helping someone other than yourself, it is the highest form of service and honor to be given. You are here so that you can help the world know better how to live here and enjoy the gift of life as you experience the same from the world.

        In some unified way, we are all one. Only with different names, addresses, stories, experiences, and backgrounds are we distinguished one from another. It is time for you to start living again for the entire creation. I remind you to please leave your legacy on the shelf so that I can leave mine next to yours as we all remember that it was only given to us for a little while.

12

The Reason for the Journey

Having found possession of truths, one can no longer be denied answers; thus, the journey is for me to someday triumph!

Awareness is achieved in life time. From birth to completion there lies in between *distance*. No one really knows the distance between life and completion; however, there are questions and answers along the distance. The major insight of the triumph reveals secrets of the world along with secrets of the self. The explanation released in the triumph suggests that everyone has been given a *distance* which exists between his/her beginning and ending, and within that distance are truth, falsity, clarity, and understanding. It holds the secrets of the world and the meaning of life.

The major insight of the triumph was cited years ago by the prophet who said, "God's thoughts are not like our thoughts and God's ways are higher than ours; for as high as the Heaven is from the earth, so are my ways." The prophet Isaiah with this timeless awareness released to us the reason for our pilgrimage on earth. What is to be gained from his wisdom is that we have an unknown distance or block of time to discover our thoughts and our ways and to discover God's thoughts and God's ways.

Then, we are accountable after we have located the truths from both ends. The journey within the self is the return to higher meaning which God intends for your life to reflect. On the journey of life, it is each of our assignments to come to what I call *knowing*.

Without experienced observation of yourself and higher meaning, how will you ever find out the reason for which you were given a distance in time? Each person is solely responsible for determining what is real and what is not real in his or her life and what truly exists about himself or herself as it relates to life. The truth is the ultimate goal for the journey and triumph. The truth hands out an understanding that finalizes curiosity about oneself and God. I have watched many people attempt to define the meaning of

The Reason for the Journey

life and I have heard so many miss the mark. The journey is all of human beings to explore, and the meaning of life is all of human beings to answer. There is no one answer. All the answers make the one answer. So far, reading this book has not been challenging until now.

The journey of the triumph is no one person's to achieve; instead, it is all persons' to identify. The truth about yourself and God is part of understanding that life is for the purpose of experiencing God in you. Every person will have a different experience. God put all of us here to be different, but God wants our differences not to separate us from our unity as human beings. We are all different examples of God. I know by now that you may be saying, "That's difficult to understand." It doesn't have to be difficult to understand. As the prophet suggested, God's ways are higher than yours. So this means that you must seek a higher meaning to life than your own.

Understanding this premise suggests that understanding has to be seen as the skill to comprehend insightfulness above your own reasoning. The journey is for your very own story to be published as part of the human being story

The Reason for the Journey

some day as a book of life. I discovered from the insight of the prophet Isaiah that God wants our reasoning to take us as far as it can take us and then allow God to resolve all that we lack in reference to knowing. In the process of finding God, we lose our ego along the way so that we aren't the final authority in our lives. This is most important about our personal journey.

I remember one day when reading the Bible, I came to the place where Jesus Christ was crying. He felt forsaken. He asked God in words, "Why has thou forsaken me?" It was at the crucifixion. Well, the story concludes that Jesus ceased crying and then came an awesome last explanation, "Lord, not my will but your will be done." Do you think that Jesus was quickened to the prophet Isaiah's insight about God's ways being higher, or do you think He was rejected of God? I choose to believe the first is true.

The journey of life and the triumph are to teach us to understand that our lives prepare the lives of others coming behind ours and that we are examples of God. Jesus Christ was an example of God and so are you! I am certain that God wants to take us beyond ourselves, and that is the reason for the journey of the triumph. So much

The Reason for the Journey

depends on one's readiness to go beyond one's thinking as the prophet has put it. It reminds us of the main insight of the triumph being a shift in consciousness or a spiritual awakening. Having a spiritual awakening is the essence of going beyond oneself to discover what lies beyond reason. The message of the insight of the prophet Isaiah about God's ways reminds me of what I have not seen, what I do not know, and how nothing can be singled out of any equation when the mind reflects God!

Once you realize that the mind of God is inhabitable, you are closest to the Observer that rules all souls--God! The distance between your birth and completion has but a time to observe so many things. It observes daily a new world emerging with new people entering it from all around the world. The world is always emerging, and it can no longer escape the sojourner who views it from a higher meaning. Every sojourner sees the world conquered from an introspective reality and higher meaning just as the prophet credited to God. So far in this book, I have not excluded you from the world in terms of death. Reason being the journey is about your removing death before the end of your distance.

The Reason for the Journey

Eternal life is seen as something that you take out of this life with you as opposed to waiting to receive it at death. Now you are wondering how to remove death from your life. To begin, erase death from your memory. Your thoughts dictate death when you think that you are dying. Your thinking should never embrace death rather completion of your journey for the next journey of higher meaning. Death inhabits the mind that does not see life beyond one's mind. Each time that I have thought about dying, I envision thinking patterns associated with no more life in contrast to seeing death as another phase of life.

The reason for the journey is to give your life meaning not equated with death. Should there be not stigma of death in your mind, there can be a new meaning of death replacing what you had once perceived as an end of reality. Every one of us on the earth is on a journey. How long the journey is, no one can be for certain. There is one thing certain which is not deniable; our lives are intertwined with God in them.

The journey reminds us how to be influenced by higher meaning instead of a local meaning. God does not want you fascinated with

The Reason for the Journey

death, instead life. In the triumph, all indication points to going beyond life and death in order to reach another reality and/or capacity of immortality. Your life can take on a new meaning when your reality of life and death is new. Once you learn how to identify life and death with higher meaning, something happens for you. You stop fearing living and dying.

You just enjoy being in the distance or eternity present and eternity past. By now, you are probably wondering if Heaven and Hell are left out of the journey. No. God can assure you! I can just tell you that I am just enjoying being in the distance between both heaven and hell called the *now.* All the answers about a life beyond now are not for your mind to reconstruct, but you should allow your vision for here and hereafter to structure your mind. In some way, death is a manipulation of the present in terms of mind control.

The journey of your life must take you back deep within your consciousness where your life began so that you find out that God gave you life to envision and make of it what you wanted and at the completion of it, discover that you have

The Reason for the Journey

always been on a journey back from where you originated, *either in God or in the void!*

13

There Are Seasons in Your Life

To define my life holistically, it is composed of many seasons because all of my experiences are in between the distance of my beginning and finishing.

There is a season for everything in your life which rotates around wisdom, knowledge, and understanding. Various stages of your development come as a result of an intellectual enhancement. I prefer to use the term shift from one position of reality to a new position of reality. Everything in your life rotates when you begin to shift your reality. In the triumph of life, we move toward the insights of life itself as we understand that reality escalates over time. According to necessary experiences and life changes, the

There Are Seasons in Your Life

course of your reality shifts many times during its entire adventure. To every challenge, new born reality awaits. Life itself is just an experience, and while we live, we exist between the distance of our beginning and ending. Each time you are experiencing growth, the insight of the triumph suggests that you are being asked to raise the bar on your existing reality.

In seasons in your life, you are developing experiences of life. The adventure of life is of such that you live it and develop with it at the same time. In every development, there's a lesson being taught, and this is the work of the triumph. Only those who endure the lessons of life really do triumph. Many of the struggles in your life are more profitable than injurious to you. Just think back as a baby when you had fallen during the process of learning how to walk. Each time you made a step toward walking, you were learning how to walk. Things like what to do and what not to do appeared in the whole process of falling down and getting back up.

There will be parts of your life when things are not so easy to accomplish. At such time just remember not to quit. Learning seasons are among the times when you are most fragile and

There Are Seasons in Your Life

discontent with moving on to the next season. I remind you, to everything there is a season for everything to happen during the course of your waking up to life and evolving. There is a season of failure and success; losing and winning; up and down; slow and fast; comfort and discomfort; low and high; projection and evaluation; praying and meditating; repeating and graduating; but all these seasons must be examined for the education they bring into your experience.

I go on to say, "You must not be alarmed by circumstances you are mastering because you are the master of all of them." Each season is for your benefit and never to harm you. Triumph is taking everything in each season in stride. In other words, everything that you experience during the seasons of your life is there for you to accomplish a specific knowing so that you can master your life as you evolve. Anytime that you evolve from one intellectual capacity to another, what you have learned is how to either adapt or climb higher than your challenge. At the turn of each season, your mind calculates all that you need to remember from that season. Ultimately, your personal triumph is embraced by seasons that are

There Are Seasons in Your Life

part of your life to make you evolve.

I will share a personal experience here. I never knew how I would handle difficulty or lack until I had experienced those times in my life. I knew what I believed that I would or would not do but it was all talk until I was challenged. For me, seasons are part of everyone's evolution.

Seasons in your life impart awareness and are necessary in the gradual process in which you change or develop more into the character of God so that you may enhance all life around you. In some ways, I am inclined to believe that seasons are indicators of where to find God. The culture of the world someday will find its way back to its Creator, and the triumph is the way thereof for everyone.

As one becomes more enlightened to the triumph, what one discovers is that life is not physical only; rather it has need for a consciousness beyond physical. I say, it has need for a divine consciousness. The entire triumph suggests that each insight that life releases points to a higher meaning of the divine consciousness needed to give life, support life, and sustain life. Let it direct you when it takes you beyond physical realms. I suggest that you try to perceive your life

There Are Seasons in Your Life

not as vapor instead as a gift to the world because everyone that knows you depends on your well being in some certain way as their own. People genuinely care about what you are going through.

There are some exceptions, but do not focus on those persons who do not want to support life and uplift human beings globally. To see your life for what it has to offer you, try to envision what it would be if you had not the opportunity to live among all that is here and now. There will be some bumps in the road in your life, but that is why you strive for life.

It comes with good and bad and that in itself is a reality of the triumph. Most of all your triumph comes along with the occurrences characterized by certain periods in which your wisdom expanded due to current and recurrent activity in your life. I know that from time to time all people get impatient with life. I am the first to admit that I sometimes do, too, pending what season I am experiencing. I found some very nice inspiration to be reassuring to me when I read the Bible. Listen to these profound words of encouragement for strength penned by the Apostle Paul, *"For in due season, we shall reap if we faint not."*

There Are Seasons in Your Life

Although many people now days have abandoned the Bible to satisfy their own cravings, this single piece of inspiration brought the triumph to full circle. What is clear about this insight is that it points to the way of triumph. In the process of triumph, one must never lose focus of the victory of life being, *if you faint not, you are victorious!*

Let me encourage you the reader of this insight more. You are able to endure anything in your life. Your endurance is discovered as you begin to see God in your seasons training you to improve and enhance your divine character so that in keeping with time, you are your own mind calendar. You won't need to be controlled by predictions to come or anything like fear. Your seasons endured are the prophecy of your life and nothing else can guide you better.

Seasons in your life prepare you for triumph. Equally important, all these occurrences such as giving birth, ceasing to live, setting or placing, taking life, recovering life, constructing, reconstructing, laughing, crying, humoring, romancing, partying, dancing, gaining, losing, giving, receiving, embracing, detaching, keeping, letting go, speaking, keeping silent, loving,

There Are Seasons in Your Life

despising, and fighting are all seasons with which to observe human courses. No person can escape the seasons that every generation passes to the next to resolve; seasons are occurrences that one must face instead of running away.

Once you confront your season, it has to release what you need to overcome it. I would agree with most people who have said life is challenging. What I agree with most about challenge is that you can't grow or evolve without some challenge in your life. If life was any way different from what it is, it would not be life at all.

We have to consider the good with the bad, the bitter with the sweet, the cold with the heat, the rain with sunshine, the love with hate, peace with war, life with death, planting with plucking, breaking down with building up, weeping with laughing, mourning with celebrating, casting stones with gathering stones, and refraining with embracing because all these happenings are the sum of life.

In the triumph, life is viewed as one adventure being experienced with various parts. Live by knowing that the crooked cannot be made

There Are Seasons in Your Life

straight and the straight crooked. Rather know that both are part of one phenomenon, life.

14

Discipline

He that can observe life without being tempted by it shall be beloved by it!

From day to day, you are interacting with all things that are within your presence and all of what is in your mind. To begin, there are so many dreams, goals, ambitions and so many other desires bombarding your heart for attention. One of the challenging aspects of life is never to become impatient. It seems that everything is so important at the time it enters your mind. This creates a temptation to manifest every want immediately. Unfortunately, life does not come with instant manifestation. Sometimes waiting is the only source of manifestation. Thus, life is tempted by overwhelming cravings and/or

Discipline

desires. He that cannot be tempted to consume of that his heart indulges is one of discipline. I have learned that discipline is the role of the triumph. I have heard it said so many times that patience is a virtue, and he that has it shall endure life. During the times in your life that you are fighting with cravings and/or desires, you seem to emotionally be attached to whatever it is that you want.

One of the lessons learned in life to be sustained is discipline. At some point, you will need it to surrender suffering. Nothing can take the place of discipline when it comes to cutting out desire. Discipline works for you like no medication can in terms of ridding you of anxiety. Too many specific wants unfulfilled create anxiety. Only discipline of your projections and abandonment of excessive desires can solve your uneasiness about things in your life. Without disciplining your heart, you will resort to troubling states of mind. You cannot afford to be worried at any time of your life.

When apprehension leads to anxiety, you are a candidate for discipline. Nevertheless, anything that you give your emotions because you crave or desire it causes you to be controlled and or tempted by it. This is never good. It is asking for

Discipline

a breakdown mentally.

This means that should your desire intensify without having it disciplined, you open the door to a state of disabling apprehension, uncertainty, and fear caused by anticipation of what you want and do not have. And when this happens, so do feelings of shame, disappointment, insecurity, and helplessness come. Your goal in life is never to become consumed by your desires. This is the purpose for which discipline is regarded as high as medications.

Over a period of time, one's desires can manipulate one's well being if not disciplined. On the other hand, discipline rewards you with a capacity and quality of being patient. Discipline is the tolerance which overcomes hardship, difficulty, or inconvenience without complaint. Wow! Don't we all need discipline to be part of our lives daily? Reason being, discipline emphasizes calmness, self-control, and the willingness or ability to endure delay. One must know that lack of discipline is the enemy of triumph; therefore, one's behavior of patience will achieve more than one's trial. It will achieve long-suffering. It suggests restraint from temptation.

Every human being needs the substance

Discipline

that only comes from discipline which is bearing or enduring pain, difficulty, provocation, or annoyance with calmness. Discipline comes as a result of having gone through certain seasons where you learned to experience yourself and God. After a series of previous occurrences that you've overcome in your life, you are then capable of calmly awaiting an outcome or result not hasty or impulsive.

There are times when you and I both are all but calm during those times that we have no choice but to wait for certain favorable outcomes. For me, these are times that I focus more on discipline and ask myself questions like what must I do to endure everything that I am having to wait on in my current season?

Often I would say to myself, there is nothing that you can do but wait for your manifestation to come or wait for your change to come. Recently, I discovered that discipline is not only waiting for a change to come but doing a few things while waiting. Here are some things that are to be included with discipline. Discipline must embrace viewing examples of other persons that have gone through your experience.

Discipline

When you view the experience of others, there is an insight released called evaluation. At such time, you tend to find calm. You are able to contrast your impatience with facts. Most times the facts are reassuring enough to encourage you to make necessary adjustments to your impatience. Others that witness your career and/or goals usually assist or motivate you to get rid of your hindrances for success and stay the course.

Next, discipline turns over the insight of patience which is a type of freedom from emotional agitation. I suggest meditation and prayer to assist you with being patient. In the process of meditation and prayer, you can enter into states of being equivalent to completely or nearly motionless which are always mind soothing. In the patient realm, you become undisturbed, and this renders you serenity, tranquility, and peace.

What is more, discipline turns over the insight of faith. You will need faith to prevent yourself from mental breakdown. Faith is really a shift in consciousness from hopelessness. Many times faith is the subjection of oneself to do all that will be necessary to bring about his/her hopes. This is not to see that your view is

Discipline

independent of other people's decisions because your view has all to do with other people's responses the majority of the time.

Lastly, discipline hands over the insight of endurance. The discipline of the triumphant is never to quit in the process of triumph. Should one quit in the process, one will conclude any hope of triumph. Self control is the triumph function. Life has endless rewarding experiences once you master your own will independent of people, circumstances, and desires. What to do about your insecurities is brought to closure in the discipline of the triumph. The triumph is the way of securing your disturbance of any sort. *Before honor is humility*... These powerful words of King Solomon solidify the power of discipline. Before you can be seen as an honorable and admirable person, you must let your humility do the work for you.

I have embraced the notion that strength is not revealed when there is an absence of challenge, but the opposite is true. Strength is revealed clearly during the time of challenge to discipline. No noteworthy person is recognized without having endured some challenge of his or her time. Furthermore, strength is revealed during

Discipline

periods wherein your patience is being tested. Discipline is the anchor of the triumph because it brings to full circle evaluation of the inner-self.

Discipline, therefore, is seen as a means of determining an outcome, quality, or truth about one's reality of life. The peak experience of the triumph is reaching a reality of observing everything in your life without being threatened by what your eyes see, your ears hear, your heart ponders, and what comes and goes through your hands. When you can defeat every imaginary foe that surfaces anywhere within your senses, you have reached the climax or the triumph.

It is not how fast one triumphs that determines how knowledgeable one is; instead, it's knowing that the triumph is a daily journey. One must interpret the triumph as his or her ongoing process evolving daily.

15

Handing Over the Kingdom of Heaven

The Kingdom of Heaven is at your hand.

At your finger tips is a degree of perfection reachable within your being and a divine consciousness which it regulates. Deeply within that sort of mystical realm, sovereignty is handed over to its seeker and, therefore, the triumph. It is the kingdom of Heaven. If I am to place emphasis on the insight of the Kingdom of Heaven, I am to thank Jesus Christ for bringing the insight out of its womb. The best way to reach into the kingdom is to allow your consciousness to reform how you are processing and interacting with yourself, everyone you meet, and all things associated with

Handing Over the Kingdom of Heaven

your inner nature. The Kingdom of Heaven holds the awareness of triumph because it hands over the insightfulness to connect human being nature to the divine nature.

Thus, we can begin to deal with ourselves with correction that unites us closer to God than our own normal standards. Jesus Christ coined the Kingdom of Heaven as the tool for transcendence in a non-spiritual culture during His time among those with whom He associated. By now, you should be able to see that the triumph is the knowledge of the Kingdom of Heaven.

Every aspect of your life, if evaluated to a divine consciousness, should open the door for your entrance into the Kingdom of Heaven so that you may understand deeper intuition about your inner potential. The focus of the triumph is the same with the exception of realigning your mind to surrender to its grander partner, your evolving consciousness.

By so doing, you prepare yourself to receive infinite awareness, wisdom, clarity, knowledge, and intuition. The triumph presents to you a shift in consciousness as opposed to a shift in time, place and body. When it comes right down to improving the way you think, nothing can be more

Handing Over the Kingdom of Heaven

contributing than your escalated consciousness which is handed down from the Kingdom of Heaven. Every insight of the Triumph was given me from the Kingdom of Heaven.

I would like for you to believe that you, too, can access the Kingdom of Heaven. To begin, you want to abort your own ideology about what you think to be wrong or right and instead focus on allowing yourself to be guided and driven by the awareness of the Kingdom of Heaven that does not restrict you in any way, no matter the intention.

If you are sick, the awareness brings healing. If you are fearful, the awareness brings faith. If you are weak, the awareness brings strength. If you are dying, the awareness brings life. If you are hungry, the awareness brings food. If you are naked, the awareness manifests clothes. If you are jobless, the awareness brings you employment.

No matter the need, the awareness handed down from the Kingdom of Heaven supplies. What other message could Jesus have been introducing to the uninformed, than that you allow your mind to surrender to a consciousness illuminated by spirit, the Spirit of God. I have been a student of

Handing Over the Kingdom of Heaven

Jesus Christ for now above 21 years, and my research points to a shift in consciousness for total access into the Heaven. In this process, total awareness can be handed over.

Truly, I am a believer of unity consciousness with God. Access comes by consciousness, mindfulness, awareness, understanding, knowledge, intuition, intention, imagination, faith, belief, etc. How else can you claim God? What you want to remember is that Jesus and God shared unity consciousness; therefore, you may, too. Let this mind be in you.

Never doubt what you can become. You are capable of the worlds being handed over to you if you can become the one willing to be its example as was Jesus through the process of unity consciousness. Haven't you heard the saying that *I am only human* usually after someone has been pointed out for some special thing done wrong in his or her life? Well, what the triumph suggests is that human being nature can reach a grander nature, the nature of God. For all of those that disbelieve it, likely it is because of how you have been trained to identify God.

I would like for you to understand God better since you have read this book. My only

Handing Over the Kingdom of Heaven

advice to you is for you not to complicate God! Once you see God as not complicated rather Spirit, you can begin to align yourself with the flow of unity consciousness and come right into the oneness or presence of God. Let me share one more insight with you about the Kingdom of Heaven. Suppose that you were capable of living a life not detached from the shades of human being. How do you suppose it would be identified?

Well, I believe that it would be a life of spirit. The practice of triumph is to live as human and spirit all at the same time. I believe that is what Jesus did. It is that awareness that the kingdom of Heaven holds and if at the time that you are ready to enter, you will possess it within, all that you have ever wanted to see God do, all that you have ever wanted to hear God say, all that you have envisioned God's doing, all that you have read about God's doing, all that you hope God to do, and all that you want to be part of in the Kingdom of Heaven. God suddenly is handing it over into your hands via awareness within and a bond of unity.

Handing Over the Kingdom of Heaven

16

Triumphant

Those who find my wisdom are they who apply my knowing, which comes from God.

- Triumph is unfolding clarity that invites you to examine the truth about your inner self; and what you may find within it are the motions of your life.
- There is clarity about the various disguises that kept us once blind to the real source of growth, enlightenment, and change.
- You can take control over inner motions to bring about the changes that you need to occur for you for any real triumph in your life.
- Triumph emphasizes awareness that enables you to see any distraction of real motions within.
- Ignorance in any area of your intellect often poses itself as a type of disguise, even subliminal when

Triumphant

- adequate awareness is needed to prevent you from experiencing emotional debilitation and/or immobilization.
- The surest way to victory is to become insightful of what you have allowed emotionally to wrap itself around your inner self.
- Studying oneself is the best possible way to triumph.
- The real reality of triumph is that you cannot deal with your weakness until you are ready to see your inner self for what you have become over the period of your life.
- Triumph comes only when you reorganize, reprioritize, realign, and reprogram your inner self because your inner self is your life living within a physical body.
- The triumph is the self having reached awareness with which to control every living motion that makes up the inner self and thus, your life is regained from acting out in ignorance.
- It is the knowledge of triumph that you are here to find.
- Your goal must never be to sort the religions out in terms of priority in your mind, instead, appreciate the truths found among all of them.

Triumphant

- The reality of all religions is that they in some way account for bringing all people to where they are now relative to knowing the Divine. Your next step then is to assess the Divine for yourself since what others discovered is not your very own discovery.
- The road leading to the triumph is plagued with ignorance, and you must be the one to turn yourself over to the Voice of higher consciousness which comes to release you from the big IGNORANCE.
- You are put here as a part of a matrix to find out certain things and leave them behind in the grand scheme of the human being so that mankind can find his way back to his Creator as you do.
- What you must know about higher consciousness is that it exists within you although it must be awakened by both good and bad things.
- Your purpose becomes clear to you after you discover your inner self.
- Nothing about seeking yourself can harm you; rather it will release the insight that you will need for the awareness of triumph to come to you.
- It is part of your destiny to discover yourself

Triumphant

first in life. Finding your way to that answer leads you to triumph.
- Discovering your true enemy is a process, but it doesn't have to be life-long; rather it's your readiness and willingness to ask yourself the right questions that expedite awareness of your ignorance which is the enemy.
- When you are truthful to yourself, you release your consciousness to bring out more truth because you are ready to face it.
- Any resistance to going beyond your fear is a setback towards the triumph.
- The triumph is designed to propel the inner self to its complete height. The triumph is the journey split into three paths: awareness, understanding and knowledge. Then, only then can we erase the big IGNORANCE
- In the process of the triumph, you will begin to discover intellectual brilliance.
- The shift in consciousness is the whole matter of the triumph.
- All of us are capable of brilliance.
- Your brilliance is attached to a shift in consciousness; therefore, you become

Triumphant

closer than you have ever been to the one reality-triumph.
- Never are you to think that you do not need other people and their experiences. To do so becomes a setback to the entire progress of bringing yourselves to the triumph.
- The brilliance of your life is measured by the answers that you have found by questioning the purpose of your life.
- One simple way to define a miracle is to see it as a shift in consciousness.
- The whole idea of the one reality of the triumph is to observe all things as if you are all and all are in you.
- Through keen observation, insight of the mysterious is released and nothing can hide From diligent observation when one asks for it, seeks it and knocks on its door without ceasing.
- Triumph is all about erasing mental and spiritual mistakes.
  Mental and spiritual conflicts wage war on the reality of your mindset.
- Struggle with the demons is at the same time struggle with alignment of the inner self.

Triumphant

- Once you erase your fears about what can plague you and once you replace your reality with believing that you can mentally and spiritually recreate yourself, there will be nothing to prevail against you.
- Mental and spiritual balance destroys your demons. In the grand scheme of things a demonic activity is the reflection of your mind out of control.
- The work of destroying your demons is the process of sorting out and cleaning up imbalanced thoughts, in order to balance the different types of inner conflict, learned behavior, restricted tendencies, and torment due to some form of captivity lingering in your thinking pattern.
- The triumph is ever creating each new moment for you to come closer to abstracting from the fear of being in a state of unity consciousness with God rather than being God.
- The worst evil controls from an unconscious state of having freewill to exercise individuality.
- Triumph is an adventure that enlightens the mind, soul, and spirit.
- Mind deception renders you the worst ruin, pain, deception, and injury.

Triumphant

- Triumph is to know that you posses all and not be tempted to be all because you know that all is in you and flows through you.
- The world is within your heart because your heart embraces the world according to your thoughts about the world.
- The mind of God is the mind that thinks the way no man has ever thought!
- Brand new thoughts always bring brand new responses into the world. Not to mention, brand new thoughts bring brand new actions into the world.
- A brand new thought, one that has not ever been given to anyone before you, is the beginning of new creation.
- I am sure that evil has its role to play in your personal triumph; therefore, I say that you don't have to be afraid of evil.
- You do not have to fear evil because you gain wisdom through experiencing it. You therefore, learn how to make adjustments in your mind and memory.
- In the triumph, evil is seen for what it really is, misfortune.

Triumphant

- The moment that you allow desire to set in your heart it longs and request for permanence. This means that whatever you allow your heart to embrace, the more your heart does not expect for you to change it.
- Discipline protects your heart from the ruin of want and/or desire.
- Nothing affects every aspect of your life as do your emotions.
- Your emotions are identifiers that reveal how you are interacting with every meaning of your life.
- This key victory to understanding yourself helps you to recover yourself from your wounds created by your emotions.
- Emotions are impulsive.
- It is necessary to give careful observation to your emotions so that you can get a grip on life in terms of what you should be holding on and/or letting go.
- Whereas, your emotions are part of your conscious, God's spirit is the makeup of your conscious!
- When you introspectively analyze your errors in consciousness, you gain awareness on how to realign yourself with abundant

Triumphant

consciousness that shifts your outlook around and assists you with new insights to produce new outcomes in your life.
- The triumph reveals that subliminal seduction's leading one away from self examination leaves oneself locked outside of revelation which leads to abundance.
- The goal in the triumph is to slow your mind down in order to observe what you blame so that you can see that the real blame is mistakes in consciousness; therefore, a shift in your consciousness is all that you need to regain vitality and regain acceleration to discovering your own person abundance.
- Experience is the instructor that assists you along the triumph.
- Experiencing yourself is the lesson of the triumph because every aspect of your life is a reflection of yourself interacting with everything that you allowed to live within you.
- The truth about yourself and God is part of understanding that life is for the purpose of experiencing God in you.
- The journey of life is all of human beings to explore, and the meaning of life is all of human

Triumphant

- beings to answer. There is no one answer. All the answers make the one answer.
- There is a season for everything in your life which rotates around wisdom, knowledge, and understanding.
- Everything in your life rotates when you begin to shift your reality.
- Life itself is just an experience and during the time that we live, we are existing between the distance of our beginning and ending.

- Each time you are experiencing growth, the insight of the triumph suggests that you are being asked to raise the bar on your existing reality.
- Ultimately, your personal triumph is embraced by seasons that are part of your life to make you evolve.
- The adventure of life is of such that you live it and develop with it at the same time.
- Seasons in your life impart awareness and are necessary in the gradual process in which you change or develop more into the character of God so that you may enhance all life around you.
- The entire triumph suggests that each insight that life releases points to a higher meaning of the

Triumphant

divine consciousness needed to give life, support life, sustain life, and give direction when it takes you beyond physical realms.
- He that can observe life without being tempted by it shall be beloved by it!
- Discipline is the role of the triumph.
- Discipline works for you like no medication can in terms of ridding you from anxiety.
- Discipline emphasizes calmness, self-control, and the willingness or ability to endure delay.
- Discipline comes as a result of having gone through certain seasons where you learned to experience yourself and God.
- You will need faith to prevent yourself from mental breakdown. Faith is really a shift in consciousness from hopelessness.
- Discipline hands over the insight of endurance.
- The discipline of the triumphant is never to quit in the process of triumph.
- Before honor is humility.
- Discipline is the anchor of the triumph because it brings to full circle evaluation of the inner-self. Discipline, therefore, is seen as a means of determining the presence, quality, or truth about one's reality of life.

Triumphant

- At your finger tips is a degree of perfection reachable within your being and a divine consciousness with which it regulates.
- Deeply within that sort of mystical realm, sovereignty is handed over to its seeker and therefore, the triumph. It is the kingdom of Heaven.
- The Kingdom of Heaven holds the awareness of triumph because it hands over the insightfulness to connect human being nature to the divine nature.
- The best way to reach into the kingdom is to allow your consciousness to reform how you are processing and interacting with yourself, everyone you meet, and all things associated with your inner nature.
- The focus of the triumph is the same as realigning your mind to surrender to its grander partner, your evolving consciousness.
- Once you see God as not complicated rather Spirit, you can begin to align yourself with the flow of unity consciousness and come right into the oneness or presence of God.

Epilogue

When writing this book, bringing relevant awareness into a world so vast was the intention. I was seemingly open to Spirit without drawing lines of separation between my higher self and the role that God served within me. Many of the insights in the book are on the living cutting edge of the emergence of a lasting triumph, one having been tutored by the consciousness of God.

The book is typical of one being inspired to reach beyond the normal functions of human being nature to discover much deeper potential by interpreting life's journey as one conceptualizes further reaches of consciousness. I was inspired to include in the book many personal insights of my own journey in consciousness. The line of thinking in the book is that of observing mistakes in consciousness, thus, recreating oneself mentally and discovering one's true meaning of life.

This work hopefully can spark a radical shift in consciousness within you in order to bring you to the next dimension of yourself and all the possibilities that come along with a new you. This book, the journey to triumph, is the way to live life. I make direct references to various eras in

Epilogue

history and persons from past dispensations while comparing and contrasting past, present, and future evolution of human being. My hope is that you enjoy reading the book and that you become another personal triumph.

With all the distractions to triumph, it is certain to present its awareness in the quiet space of your mind. Overall, the triumph is a journey to happiness certain to happen during your life. Only those who will treasure its wisdom and direction are rewarded the peaceful destiny. Discover the meaning of life and value as you allow yourself to triumph.

Summary

This book is about how one transforms and interprets what has been present for generations on his/her journey triumph. It contains much of the insights of the self and God within whom the self exists. The language placed in the book is the language of triumph bringing people out from mind control of all things to merely a reflection of one's experiences and expressions, emerging as a being empowered with new possibilities, potential, and consciousness.

Much of the content of the book is direct biblical quotes although insight from all that I have been exposed to in the realm of spirit summarizes the vast majority of the text. Ideals about how to recreate oneself consciously seems to be the greater example of the book. Much of the reverberation throughout the book is the reality of triumph empowering the self with awareness, recovering ultimate understanding, and equipping the self with timeless knowledge for a grander life and success via techniques about how to rearrange your thoughts, feelings, and perception of life. A great deal of energy that permeates the book focused on confronting oneself in terms of choices, beliefs, cultural

Summary

norms, mind control and freedom. Almost every attempt to bring you closer to the ultimate reality of existing inside the infinite consciousness of God is what the book portrays.

It highly embraces liberated actions for experiencing life freely, responsibly, and intentionally while at the same time letting your meaning of life emerge from the vast experiences that make it. With this in mind, the holistic meaning of life is to triumph beyond the resistance to know yourself to a grander degree by understanding how to develop the self to reach total awareness of those things occurring in your life. Thus, living has to be designed for moving all people to advanced stages of inner awareness to keep the soul evolving.

Sections of the book bring to the front a brand new way of reconstructing your life using the power of shift in consciousness to experience desired results. Ultimately, the reality of the triumph is the surest way of understanding how to become insightful of what you have allowed emotionally to wrap itself around your inner self, thus, making precision adjustments which lead you to become a victor as you reach deeper within the Infinite Source-God!

Bibliography

King James Reference Bible

Copyright 2000, Zondervan Publishing,

Grand Rapids, Michigan, U.S.A.

Library of congress Card Number 00-75836

The American heritage College *dic.tion.ar.y*

Third Edition

Copyright 1993 by Houghton Mifflin Company

Other Books by Dr. Dwayne Gavin

MORALITY- The book contains many secrets to enhance you to reach your fullest potential via a shift in consciousness. Wisdom from across the earth comes together in unity within the book as it contains integration of spirituality, psychology, and philosophy. The book has no religious prejudice. The focus of the book is to heighten global human being with an emphasis on higher reality.

CHOOSE YOUR LIFE- Choose your life is the wisdom of generational truths. The book contains thousands of years of quotes from people who have shaped the world with a global awareness. The work offers an approach to attain new outcomes in one's life in a very relevant way in a modern, faced-pace culture. The book offers logical, philosophical, and psychological approaches to decision making.

See Dr. Dwayne Gavin Awareness for Life Broadcast © sponsored by DG PUBLISHING HOUSE. dwaynegavin.com. Dr. Dwayne Gavin's teachings help you reach your fullest potential to create extraordinary results in your life, career, business and organization. His insight on the fundamentals of coaching is a tool to assist you to mentally recreate yourself to produce greater manifestations to happen in your life. Dr. Gavin's book titled CHOOSE YOUR LIFE is one of two manuals for motivational speaking, coaching, teaching, counseling and inner empowerment.

Follow me on twitter.com for daily inspiration or dwaynegavin.com

www.ingramcontent.com/pod-product-compliance
Lightning Source LLC
Chambersburg PA
CBHW070804100426
42742CB00012B/2243